W9-BRK-347

Twayne's United States Authors Series

Sylvia E. Bowman, *Editor*

INDIANA UNIVERSITY

Bruce Jay Friedman

Bruce Jay Friedman

By MAX F. SCHULZ
University of Southern California

813.
54
FRIEDMAN

 219

Twayne Publishers, Inc.   ::   New York

78-05350

Copyright © 1974 by Twayne Publishers, Inc.
All Rights Reserved

Library of Congress Catalog Card Number: 72-9347

ISBN 0–8057–0290–3
MANUFACTURED IN THE UNITED STATES OF AMERICA

Preface

Bruce Jay Friedman talks quietly, seriously, and sensibly about literature, with almost none of the stylized, "gap-popping" dialogue that is the hallmark of his fiction. Although not formally schooled in the Western literary tradition, he is deeply knowledgeable of his fictional kinships and can discourse movingly and meaningfully about writers who have been tagged (not without his inadvertent complicity!) as Black Humorists.

Friedman is eminently fitted for the role of fictional and nonfictional commentator on post-World-War-II America. Except for two years in the Air Force and four years in college, he has lived all his life in New York City, which easily qualifies as a microcosm of the shifting populations; racial tensions; student riots; anti-war protests; polluted air; electric-power breakdowns; food and fuel shortages; and teacher, policeman, and public transportation strikes that afflict the world's urban centers in the television-centered, race-to-the-moon, technocrat era. He grew up during the last great decade of the Hollywood movie-star period, reached maturity during the war years, and mastered the craft of writing during the McLuhan-heralded post-Gutenberg age.

Friedman lives with ease in two worlds: (1) Great Neck, Long Island, an upper-middle-class preserve of lawyers, physicians, and psychiatrists, where he occupies a large colonial house of the 1930's vintage, full of American antiques and sundry animals, with his wife Ginger and three pre-teen-age sons, Josh, Drew, and Kipp; and (2) the upper East Side and Greenwich Village, Manhattan, current havens of the New York writing scene, show business personalities, "hippies," and assorted fringe culture dissidents, where he fraternizes in such "in" places as Elaine's and Casey's with Norman Mailer, Terry Southern, and Edward Albee.

The unrest of the 1960's is a puzzle and a worry to everyone on the heavy side of thirty. The temper of the decade has challenged a new generation of American writers to find fictional equivalents to the metaphysics of (in Norman Mailer's words) a "pill-ridden, electronically-oriented, chemically-grounded generation." Because of the nature of its affect, I decided that the first full-scale evaluation of Friedman (one of the new writers) should stress the spirit of the times rather than the biographical influences. Unquestionably, Friedman writes intuitively, in part, reaching deep into his psyche for much of his fictional material. It does not take much acumen to recognize that he has fixations (the devouring virago mother and the inconstant wife, to name two), but to hazard psychological explanations of a man just entering his forties, with half a lifetime of writing still ahead, strikes me as being, if not critically irrelevant, at least unnecessary and possibly even presumptuous. Eminently more appropriate, therefore, at this stage of Friedman's development than "Freudian" *explication de texte* is a sketching-in of the civil, intellectual, and literary ferment that provides the ambience of his fiction. My emphasis in this study is on Friedman's social consciousness as a human being and on his social realism as a writer. Nor is this emphasis wholly arbitrary, considering his training as a journalist and his active observation of the scene of the 1960's for such magazines as *Esquire, Harper's, Holiday,* and *Saturday Evening Post.*

The first chapter attempts a definition of Black Humor, as one of the most important literary developments in America at mid-century; and it places Friedman in this movement in relation to his contemporaries. Chapters 2, 3, 4, and 5 consider chronologically Friedman's fiction, and Chapter 6 his dramatic and non-fictional writings. Basically, the discussion of Friedman proceeds from the general to the particular, from history of ideas to criticism of specific works, from cultural analysis to biographical elucidation. However, the reader who would like to know about Friedman beyond the bare recitation of vital statistics in the Chronology and the brief statement about his writing habits, his early literary efforts, and his literary opinions gathered from interviews and from his unpublished writings to be found in Chapters 4 and 6 will have to wait. Friedman is but on the threshold of his middle years and critical evaluation a never-ending process.

MAX F. SCHULZ

University of Southern California

Acknowledgments

Permission to quote from *Stern, A Mother's Kisses, Black Angels,* and *Scuba Duba* copyright © by Bruce Jay Friedman, and from *Catch-22* by Joseph Heller, has been granted by Simon and Schuster, Inc.; from *Far from the City of Class* copyright © by Bruce Jay Friedman has been granted by the Robert Lantz/Candida Donadio Literary Agency; from *Black Humor* copyright © by Bantam Books, Inc.; from *The Dick* and *Steambath* copyright © by Bruce Jay Friedman has been granted by Alfred A. Knopf, Inc.; and from *Journey to the End of the Night* by Louis-Ferdinand Céline, J. H. P. Marks, Trans., copyright 1934, 1961 by Louis-Ferdinand Céline has been granted by New Directions Publishing Corporation.

Parts of chapters one and five appeared originally in *College English* and in *The Southern Review,* who have kindly consented to their reprinting here.

I wish also to express my gratitude to Dr. Paul Kay, who generously let me read two unpublished versions of a long study he has made of Friedman's *Stern.*

One final word, a note of thanks to Bruce Jay Friedman and to his wife Ginger for their graceful reception of me during a weekend spent in New York City and for patient and helpful answers to all my continuing inquiries over a period of four years. Thanks are also due to the Graduate School of the University of Southern California for financial support in the research and writing of this book.

Contents

Chronology

1930   Bruce Jay Friedman born April 26 in the Bronx in the shadow of Yankee Stadium, son of Irving and Molly (Liebowitz) Friedman.

1930–   Reared in the Bronx, corner of Sheridan Avenue and 163rd
1947   Street; attended Public School 35, Junior High School 117, and DeWitt Clinton High School.

1947–   Attended the University of Missouri; majored in journal-
1951   ism.

1951–   Served as first lieutenant in the United States Air Force,
1953   in public relations in and around St. Louis, and as correspondent, feature writer, and photographer on the staff of the Air Force magazine, *Air Training*.

1954   Married Ginger Howard from St. Louis, whom he had seen while attending the University of Missouri, but did not meet until four years later when he was in the Air Force.

1954–   Worked for Magazine Management Company, eventually
1956   as an executive editor in charge of the magazines *Men*, *Male*, and *Man's World*.

1962   Published *Stern* with Simon and Schuster, under whose imprint the first five of his books appeared.

1963   Published *Far from the City of Class*, a collection of sixteen stories.

1964   Published *A Mother's Kisses*.

1966   Quit Magazine Management Company (spring) to do a screen script (finished November) of Jock Carroll's novel, *The Shy Photographer*.

1966   Published *Black Angels*, a collection of sixteen stories.

1967   Opened (October 10) *Scuba Duba* for a long run (closed June 8, 1969) at the New Theater, New York City.

1970   Published *The Dick* with Alfred A. Knopf.

1970   Opened (June 30) *Steambath* for a four-month run (closed October 18) at the Truck and Warehouse Theater, New York City.

CHAPTER 1

Friedman as Black Humorist

I *The Fiction of Black Humor*

CONRAD KNICKERBOCKER is the theoretician of Black Humor; Bruce Jay Friedman, the field commander. Yet neither they nor their fellow partisans can agree on a common article of faith or theater of operations. Black Humor is a movement, therefore, without unity, comprised of a group of guerrillas who huddle around the same campfire only because they know that they are in Indian territory. Even though they grudgingly concur about the enemy, they anarchistically refuse to coordinate their attack. Desperate men, they have abandoned not only the safety of received opinions but also left to the news media the advance positions of satirical shock treatment; they themselves charge instead the exposed flanks of undiscovered lands "somewhere out beyond satire," which require "a new set of filters" to be seen.[1]

The irony is that Friedman inadvertently gave literary respectability and philosophical cohesion to the group when he patched together thirteen pieces (short stories and excerpts from novels, including one of his own short stories, "Black Angels") for Bantam Books in 1965 and nonchalantly entitled them *Black Humor.* The other twelve writers on whom he had perpetrated this travesty were Terry Southern, John Rechy, J. P. Donleavy, Edward Albee, Charles Simmons, Louis-Ferdinand Céline, James Purdy, Joseph Heller, Thomas Pynchon, Vladimir Nabokov, Conrad Knickerbocker, and John Barth. The venture was an exercise in bookmaking; for Friedman's novels had had good critical reception but modest sales: he had a living to earn, a family to support.

Much to Friedman's surprise, he found himself tarred with his own black label. He was indeed dumbfounded, like one of his fictional characters, to learn that someone was indeed listening; but he now regrets his part in this bit of carpentry for the trade. The tag has been applied to his own fiction until he winces when he hears the words. "What I ended up with was 13 separate writers with completely private and unique visions," he admitted with ingratiating candor as early as his foreword to the collection, "who in so many ways have nothing at all to do with one another and would not know or perhaps even understand one another's work if they tripped over it." [2]

Despite Friedman's protestations and a recent effort to describe his play *Scuba Duba* with the more critically usable phrase "tense comedy," the Black Humor tag seems to have stuck. If, however, the term is to have any critical usefulness, aside from an opaque Impressionistic meaning, it must be more clearly defined than hitherto. For, as a term, Black Humor is beguilingly vague: it fails to distinguish among the genres; it fails to differentiate the contemporary movement from the many instances in the past of similar literary reactions to human experience; and it fails to focus the means (plot, character, thought, and diction) and the end (effect on reader: laughter, tears, etc.) of literary expression, as Friedman's alternative "tense comedy" attempts more successfully to do. Indeed, Black Humor needs a definition that will be not only inclusive but exclusive.

Although several attempts have been made to define Black Humor, the results have been elusive and chimerical. (1) Despairing of any substantive formula, Friedman opts for a mystery that has been around as long as the human mind has had an iconoclastic itch to peel back disguises and to probe "thoughts no one else cares to think." [3] (2) Robert Scholes [4] tries to channel Friedman's general concern for persistent mental habits by shifting to formalist concerns and by identifying Black Humor with the recurrent intellectual reaction of artists to the limitations of realism. As with the painterly aims of some modern artists, Black Humorists, he believes, are absorbed by the possibilities of playful and artful construction. They are master fabulators in the tradition of the Romance and its baroque configurations. Like Plato's "all-in-one," Scholes's "fabulation" unfortunately becomes in practice a nondiscriminating standard, subsuming in its alembic all "artful contrivance"; for is not the artist by nature a maker of patterns?—the stark fables of Isaac Bashevis Singer as contrived as the mannered convolutions of Vladimir Nabokov? Surely Scholes's already disparate group of fabulators, ranging from Lawrence Durrell to John Hawkes, could not deny membership to the master fabulator—and ironist—Henry James. *Hic reductio ad absurdum!*

Scholes's premise of historical inclusiveness leads inevitably to self-contradiction and the negation of his thesis. If, on the other hand, Scholes sees this fabulation as a game to be enjoyed in part for its own sake, a decadence appreciated by a specially developed taste for the sophisticated, the artful—as his emphasis on Nabokov and Barth as arch-fabulators would suggest—then, of course, the earnest moral position of a Henry James or the sincere social gesture of a Bruce Jay Friedman, a Louis-Ferdinand Céline, a Terry Southern, or a Kurt Vonnegut becomes an important distinction. Scholes would not deny that Nabokov and Barth have their serious themes, or that Friedman has his estheticism; but he suggests that the ways Nabokov and Barth handle their subjects loom larger in their calculations than the stylisms of Friedman loom in his. The verbal conundrums of Nabokov and Barth in any final analysis would appear more the stance of the esthete than the verbal uniqueness of Friedman. Scholes's definition seems inevitably, therefore, to polarize the practitioners of Black Humor into at least two groups distinguishable by the formalist means they employ.

(3) Conrad Knickerbocker in his groundbreaking essay [5] diminishes the Black Humorist to *poète maudit*, an alienated artist and scorpion to the status quo, so full of the poison of self-loathing for the "specially tailored, ready-to-wear identities" given to us by television, movies, the press, the universities, the government, the military, and the business world that he mortally stings himself, pricking the surrogate skin of society.

We unnecessarily compound the problem of determining what Black Humor is when we try, like Scholes, to see it as a fixed attitude of mind, periodically emerging in the history of literature. Such an esthetic currency produces an impasse not unlike that reached by those critics who interpret Romanticism and Classicism as constant modes of apprehending human experience. More limiting, certainly, but more useful in the long run is the recognition that Black Humor is a phenomenon of the 1960's, comprising a group of writers who share a viewpoint and an esthetics for indicating the boundaries of a nuclear-powered, war-saturated, chemically oriented world.

In the 1930's a voice like Nathanael West's is shrill with frustration and disillusionment, with an outraged sense of betrayal. The ordered world of values, in which he wishes to believe, never reaches his expectations. One ideal after another is disclosed as a dream. In the 1940's and 1950's—the postwar era—the Existentialist solution to the collapse of the Christian cultural system, to the loss of God and of an identifiable moral order, dominates the scene. Metaphysical despair, it is hoped, can be cured by individual action. Writers like Saul Bellow, Bernard Malamud, and Norman Mailer accept a dwindled world, in which only personal commitment makes sense. Their vision of human loneliness remains fundamentally tragic, but their fictional method often assumes a comic mask.

In the 1960's a disoriented universe is cheerfully taken for granted. Writers like Barth, Pynchon, Nabokov, Vonnegut, and Friedman dramatize the sham of historical sequence and the self-hypnosis of individual sensibilities with unsentimental insouciance. Chance and coincidence happily reign, perched on a juggernauting technology that threatens, with computer efficiency, to reduce all life to inanimacy. In Pynchon's *V.*, "Keep cool but care," McClintic Sphere tells Paola (Chap. 12), echoed by SHROUD'S advice to Benny Profane (Chap. 13). "Cool it" emerges as the password of the decade, and the writers who surfaced during the past ten years eye life with its perspective. The prospect of personal estrangement does not terrify them, nor do they feel any overwhelming urge to resolve the questions they raise, to make even a tacit declaration of values. In this respect, they share with the dramatists of the Absurd the nihilistic assumptions of this century; and they approximate in the narrative devices of their fiction the dramatic conventions of disproportion (emphasis on trivial action), repetitive speech, and dislocation of time and space.

Like all comic visions of life, Black Humor concerns itself with social realities. In this respect, it is not anti-Realistic romance (as Scholes argues) [6] so much as realism forced to the extreme of a metaphysical truth—an intensified, at times *Sur*realistic, concentration on those details of contemporary existence that illustrate a disoriented world.

II   *The Comic Divisiveness of Individual and Society*

In the metaphysical assumptions that underlie the views of the relationship of man to society, traditional comedy and Black Humor differ radically. New Comedy, according to Northrop Frye's "The Argument of Comedy," [7] always worked toward a reconciliation between the individual and society. Either the normal individual was freed from the bonds of an arbitrary "humours" society, or a normal society was rescued from the whims imposed by "humours" individuals. As might be suspected, Frye finds lurking beneath this realignment of social forces the yearly triumph of spring over winter. He sees the victory of normality over abnormality as a formalized celebration of the archetypal pattern of death and resurrection. In the marriage of the young hero, in his triumph over the old pursuer *(senex),* in the freeing of the slave, New Comedy rehearsed the victory of life over death.

Black Humor stops short of any such victory. It enacts no individual release or social reconciliation; it often moves toward, but ordinarily fails to reach, that goal. Like Shakespeare's "dark comedies," Black Humor condemns man to a dying world; it never envisions, as do Shakespeare's early and late comedies, the possibilities of human escape from an aberrant environment into a forest milieu—the ritual of the triumph of the green world over the wasteland. Thus, at the conclusion of Bruce Jay Friedman's first novel, *Stern,* the Jewish protagonist is as alienated from his Jew-hating neighbor and from the suburban neighborhood he lives in as he was at the outset. Despite his efforts at *rapprochement,* he and society persist in the bonds of abnormality that separate each other. Similarly, in Friedman's *A Mother's Kisses,* Joseph tugs at the symbolic end of his mother's silver cord and reaches out for girls of his own age; but the gulf between him and normal sexual experience remains unbridged at the novel's conclusion. That the expanse has been shortened—that Joseph has moved away from his mother toward his contemporaries— explains in part the dim penetration of light in this novel as compared to the impenetrable blackness blanketing *Stern.* In *A Mother's Kisses* Friedman skillfully hints at an eventual release when Joseph puts his mother Meg on the train for home in the final scene and when his last encounter with a girl (in a Saturday night foray at a nearby college) ends with the interruption of someone else and not with his own timid withdrawal. Still, full adjustment of Joseph to his milieu fails to "come off" within the novel.

Marcus Klein demonstrates in his study of Bellow, Malamud, and others that the fictional heroes of the 1950's were bent on a movement from alienation to accommodation with society.[8] The 1960's hero, according to William Sherman—and he names Samson Sillitoe (in Elliott Baker's *A Fine Madness*, 1964), Yossarian (in Joseph Heller's *Catch-22*, 1955), Sebastian Dangerfield (in J. P. Donleavy's *The Ginger Man*, 1955), and McMurphy (in Ken Kesey's *One Flew Over the Cuckoo's Nest*, 1962)—seeks no such reconciliation. Sherman defines the new isolation less as alienation than as surety of survival as an individual.[9] But Sherman's list of heroes is highly selective: it conveniently ignores Friedman's Stern, Nabokov's Humbert Humbert, Vonnegut's Eliot Rosewater, Pynchon's Benny Profane, and Barth's Ebenezer Cooke, among others. Also, Sherman's definition of the new hero quietly forgets that Yossarian opts at the end of *Catch-22* for social solidarity when he decides not to betray his fellow fliers in a deal with Major Cathcart and not to let Nately's Whore's Kid Sister go the way of the other waifs of war; and that Sebastian Dangerfield hails from the early 1950's, not the mid-1960's, and, like the Angry Young Men of his time, longs for affluent respectability, for middle-class amenities, a corporation job and suburban domesticity, hot baths and country-club membership.

In actuality, in the 1960's, the search of the protagonist for accommodation with his fellow man continues; but the author of that decade no longer believes, as did the writer of the 1950's that *rapprochement* is possible. Hence, a Benny Profane drifts yo-yo fashion from group to group and from pad to pad, terrified of what transpires on the Street and in the Back Room; Humbert's pursuit of love ends in the death row; Stern's proffers of neighborliness leave him ostracized and ulcer-wracked; Eliot Rosewater's experiment in grass-roots, small-town communion precipitates a nervous breakdown; and Yossarian's tentative move toward society in his decision to rescue Nately's Whore's Kid Sister is compromised by its being also an act of desertion from the Air Force in wartime and its including the preposterous intention of escape across war-torn Europe to Sweden.

Black Humor's denial of social reconciliation or individual re-lease is epitomized in the vision of Louis-Ferdinand Céline, who "worked the same beat" (Friedman admiringly acknowledges), "thought all your thoughts . . . was dumbfounded as many times a day as you are, long before you were born." [10] In Céline's *Journey to the End of the Night* the best that the narrator-pro-tagonist Bardamu can offer as a summation of his "aimless pil-grimage" through this "truly appalling, awful world" is that "life leaves you high and dry long before you're really through." [11] With numbness of heart, Bardamu acknowledges that neither per-son nor house can speak to him, that no one can find another in the darkness through which each is condemned to travel a long way by himself, alone. Céline heralds the dead end of the eighteenth-century social and political ideal of the *philosophes* that is memorably epitomized in William Godwin's boast that society is a collection of individuals.[12] And the many Black Humorists today who regard Céline as ur-progenitor continue to push farther into the Célinesque darkness—incredible as that seems—in determined exploration of the permutability of urban existence and the paralysis of human indifference.

The divisiveness of society is certainly one consequence of the individualizing bent of Protestant humanism of the past five hundred years, but other causes peculiar to our century are equally discernible. We need only to contrast the Rome of Plautus and the London of Shakespeare with the New York City of Friedman and the Los Angeles of Pynchon to see the change in social cohesion that has taken place. The Plautean Romans and the Shakespearean Londoners were united by a common class and culture, but Friedman's New Yorkers and Pynchon's An-gelenos are connected to each other only by subways and free-ways. Although people live elbow to elbow in a fantasy known as the Urban Scene, they are separated by vast distances from the places of personal relationship: work, church, parental homes, recreation. Friedman's Everyman, Stern, daily faces a harrowing multi-houred trip to the office; and he does so among indifferent, or outright hostile, fellow commuters. Pynchon's Angelenos spend equal numbers of hours speeding down ribbons of concrete, each encased in his metal cocoon of an automobile, cut off from the intimate sounds and smells of human voices and bodies, per-mitted only the occasional blurred glimpse of a face through two panes of window glass as they whisk past one another. This is the divisive "creepy world of precardiac Mustang drivers who scream insults at one another only when the windows are up"[13] that the Black Humorist contemplates, a world in which the traditional comic reconciliation of individual and society makes little sense.

Black Humor differs also from current Existentialist views of man in refusing to treat his isolation as an ethical situation. Friedman slyly ribs Stern's effort to offset his fearful solitariness. For example, in the last scene, Stern's self-conscious embrace of wife and child in the nursery becomes a parodic tableau of family solidarity mistimed and miscued:

> Now Stern walked around the room, touching the rugs to make sure they wouldn't fall on his son's face. Then he said, "I feel like doing some hugging," and knelt beside the sleeping boy, inhaling his pajamas and putting his arm over him. His wife was at the door and Stern said, "I want you in here, too." She came over, and it occurred to him that he would like to try something a little theatrical, just kneel there quietly with his arms protectively draped around his wife and child. He tried it and wound up holding them a fraction longer than he'd intended.[14]

Céline's dry tone and Parisian argot are similarly scornful of any mask other than the comic. With a matter-of-factness that suggests the laconic air of boredom (incongruously belied by the precipitous torrent of words), Bardamu recounts his indifference to life:

> Whatever people may care to make out, life leaves you high and dry long before you're really through.
>
> The things you used to set most store by, you one fine day decide to take less and less notice of, and it's an effort when you absolutely have to. You're sick of always hearing yourself talk. . . . You abbreviate. You renounce. Thirty years you've been at it, talking, talking . . . You don't mind now about being right. You lose even the desire to hang on to the little place you've reserved for yourself among the pleasures of life. . . . You're fed up. From now on, its enough just to eat a little, to get a bit of warmth, and to sleep as much as you can on the road to nothing at all. . . . The only thing that still means anything very much to you are the little regrets, like never having found time to get

round and see your old uncle at Bois-Colombes, whose little song died away forever one February evening. That's all one's retained of life, this little very horrible regret; the rest one has more or less successfully vomited up along the road, with a good many retchings and a great deal of unhappiness. One's come to be nothing but an aged lamppost of fitful memories at the corner of a street along which almost no one passes now. (459–60)

"If you're to be bored," Bardamu concludes, "the least wearisome way is to keep absolutely regular habits." Indeed, suicide would be a nonsensical gesture of metaphysical despair or of archaic heroics. Todd Andrews reaches this decision at the end of Barth's *The Floating Opera* when he recognizes that, if there is no good reason why he should go on living, there is also no reason why he should die. The conception of a protagonist who falls short of his aspirations to the social mean, a common man *manqué*, is what makes Black Humor a somewhat limited vision capable of the specific aberrations of comedy rather than of the universal condition of tragedy.

We can gauge the degree of detachment practiced by Black Humor if we compare these examples of the genre with the contrary moral renunciation of human kind that fires Schrella's decision at the conclusion of Heinrich Böll's *Billiards at Half-Past Nine*. A fugitive from Nazi Germany, Schrella has returned to his native city after an exile of more than twenty years; but he does not plan to stay. Unlike the rest of his countrymen and such Black Humor figures as Stern, he resolutely resists accommodation with the destructive powers of the past which persevere in the forces of the present. As a continuing moral protest, he persists in his rooming house and hotel existence:

> "I'm afraid of houses you move into, then let yourself be convinced of the banal fact that life goes on and that you get used to anything in time. Ferdi would be only a memory, and my father only a dream. And yet they killed Ferdi, and his father vanished from here without a trace. They're not even remembered in the lists of any political organzation, since they never belonged to any. They aren't even remembered in the Jewish memorial services, since they weren't Jews. . . . I can't live in this city because it isn't alien enough for me. . . . My hotel room's exactly right. Once I shut the door behind me, this city becomes as foreign as all the others." (Chap. 13)

Billiards at Half-Past Nine is black enough in its vision of man; but its fervid crusade to alter human nature and its desperate rejection of society until such moral regeneration takes place give it a tragic rather than comic mask. When Böll wishes, of course, he can write Black Humor. In *The Clown* he dispassionately—even cheerfully —depicts the deterioration of Hans Schnier, a social misfit who cannot adjust to the hypocrisy of postwar Germany. Whereas Dostoevski's Idiot spirals tragically heavenward, Böll's Clown winds down through Biedermeier instances of insult to a beggar's cushion in the Bonn train station. Like the irreverently treated heroes of Vonnegut's *God Bless You, Mr. Rosewater* and of Barth's *The Sot-Weed Factor,* Schnier the "wise fool" proves to be more foolish than wise. But even at this ebb tide of his life, Schnier unlike Schrella continues to seek out human company.

Like Böll's Clown, the protagonist of Black Humor does not despair with the savage bitterness of a Miss Lonelyhearts. Nor does he remain aloof, dismissing society with cold imperviousness, like Dennis Barlow in Evelyn Waugh's *The Loved One;* instead, he worries about his place in it. Only after repeated rebuffs in his search for a relationship with others does he accept his empty existence with an angry shrug like Ferdinand Bardamu. The protagonist may be a booby like Friedman's Stern, a *naïf* like his Joseph, an anti-hero like Céline's Bardamu, a silly like Vonnegut's Eliot Rosewater, a pervert like Nabokov's Humbert Humbert, a clown like Heller's Yossarian, a fool like Barth's Ebenezer Cooke—but he is never an untouched innocent like Waugh's Paul Pennyfeather in *Decline and Fall,* nor a dismembered scapegoat like West's Lemuel Pitkin in *A Cool Million,* nor a gull like Jonathan Swift's Gulliver. At the end of *Decline and Fall,* Paul Pennyfeather returns to college unchanged by his scarifying mishaps. At the end of *A Cool Million,* Lemuel Pitkin is without thumb, leg, eye, teeth, and scalp—indeed his very existence; yet he is ironically a heroic witness to the American dream of success.

The Black Humor protagonist does not simply function, like these satiric foils, as an authorial lens for analyzing the real, corrupt object of the satire. For him detachment does not mean withdrawal from the world, as it does for Swift's Gulliver, Voltaire's Candide, or Waugh's Dennis Barlow. The central character is at once observer of and participant in the drama of dissidence; he is detached from and yet affected by what happens around him. Extremely conscious of his situation, he is radically different from the satiric puppets of Waugh and West who bounce back like Krazy Kat from every cruel flattening as smooth and round as before, their minds unviolated by experience. The Black Humor protagonist's—and the author's—gaze is more often than not inward; it is concentrated on what Conrad Knickerbocker has called the terrors and possibilities of self-knowledge.[15] His prison-house loneliness, forced upon him by existence, becomes an odyssey into being, a Célinesque journey to the end of the night.

The moral quality of society—the aim of satire—is not, according to Northrop Frye, the point of comedy and its resolution of individual and group.[16] Nor is it the objective of Black Humor, which resists any final accommodation. As Scholes notes, the Black Humorist is not concerned with what to do about life but with how to take it.[17] This statement is not meant to imply that he has no moral position but to suggest that this position is *implicit*. He may challenge the trances and hysterias of society, as Conrad Knickerbocker suggests; [18] but he does not ordinarily urge choice on us. He seeks rather a comic perspective on both tragic fact and moralistic certitude. In extreme instances—for example, in some of Kurt Vonnegut's writings—this attitude of mind leads to the novel's refusal to take its implied moral position seriously. Barth's *The Sot-Weed Factor* has been faulted for its abdication of responsibility to answer the questions it raises about intrinsic values; Heller's *Catch-22*, for its central evasiveness as regards war—for its not having a point of view, an awareness of what things should or should not be.[19] And one of the most recent of these novels, Pynchon's *The Crying of Lot 49*, formulates an elaborate historical theory as an explanation of the legacy of present-day America, only to suggest that the theory may be an enigmatic hoax perpetrated by the paranoic human mind. Such is the ultimate ethical and esthetic chaos that these novels risk in their rage for an inclusive purchase on reality.

III   *The Metaphysics of Multiplicity*

To the satirist, there are false and true versions of reality. Whispering Glades in Waugh's *The Loved One* is a false ordering of reality, but the traditionalism identified with English country houses is a true ordering. The illogicality of action rampant in the Algerian world of West's *A Cool Million* does not ultimately deny an underlying faith in the Puritan ethic of industry and perseverance. To the Black Humorist, contrariwise, all versions of reality are mental constructs; for no one of them is aprioristically truer than another. Falsity obtains only when we mistakenly assume that one verbal construct morally or intellectually preempts all others.

The Black Humorist sees life as a maze that is fragmentary and multiple, rather than unitive and conclusive. The human dilemma posed by such a view is given full voice in Barth's *The Sot-Weed Factor.* "Ah, God," Ebenezer Cooke writes to his sister,

> it were an easy Matter to choose a Calling, had one all Time to live in! I should be fifty Years a Barrister, fifty a Physician, fifty a Clergyman, fifty a Soldier! Aye, and fifty a Thief! All Roads are fine Roads, beloved Sister, none more than another, so that with one Life to spend I am a Man bare-bumm'd at Taylors with Cash for but one pair of Breeches, or a Scholar at Bookstalls with Money for a single Book; to choose ten were no Trouble; to choose one, impossible! All Trades, all Crafts, all Professions are wondrous, but none is finer than the rest together. I cannot choose, sweet Anna: twixt Stools my Breech falleth to the Ground! (Chap. 2)

Rather than acquiesce like Ebenezer into immobility before the multiplicity of choice, the Black Humorist prefers, like Ebenezer's tutor and alter ego Burlingame, to confront as many combinations of this kaleidoscope of shapes, actions, and possibilities as he can. Quantitative, not qualitative, comprehension then is his strategy, with the hope that out of this wide-angled vision, as out of a programmed computer, will issue verbal patterns meaningful to our experience.

Both Friedman and Knickerbocker—as well as James Purdy and Terry Southern—have argued, as an apologetics for the distortion of experience in their novels, that "traditional forms cannot accommodate a reality which now includes a Jack Ruby." [20] Unquestionably Black Humor reflects in its fictional forms the metaphysics of its vision. This metaphysics includes a discontinuous and instantaneous world of electronic viewing where action and consequence are monstrously disparate, as well as the psychic tension of detached involvement in that world, both of which contribute to an esthetic which down plays the traditional importance in narrative art of the consecutive, linear, and ordered grammar of plot.

The Black Humorist is a social critic, as Bruce Jay Friedman claims,[21] only in that he "lays bare" the perversions, "hang-ups," "sacred cows," and taboos of society. They may be as universal as Céline's preoccupations with the absurdity of war and institutionalized inhumanities, or as personal as Friedman's catharses of sexual blocks. That which familiarity, semantic blur, and such intellectual opiates as patriotism, sanctity of family, religious allegiance, and racial ideals have numbed us into accepting without demur as commonplace and unquestionable, the Black Humorist uncovers anew as murderous and frightening. Focusing our attention on such things, he forces us to share with him the painful laughter of examining and analyzing our mutually hidden and camouflaged obsessions. He exorcises as comical and lighthearted that from which we customarily recoil in horror. But where satire would perform a lobotomy on these sudden terrors, Black Humor simply records them for future reference, though not without a wink so tight that it brings an emphatic tear to both author's and reader's eyes. It is more a detached history of the black thoughts of the human mind and the unspoken fears of society than its scourge.

For example, Nabokov's *Lolita* documents without editorial indignation the drab and furtive bowers of Hymen that masquerade as the proud American institution, the Motel. Barth's *The Sot-Weed Factor* luxuriates in the venery and political venality of the colonial American. Friedman's *A Mother's Kisses* counts the prurient glimpses of sex by a seventeen-year-old as the boyish collecting of baseball cards; it defines the sacrosanct fellowship of father and son as a tension of day-long silence broken only by such intimacies as "I buy a paper here," "I usually stand at this end [of the subway] and hold on to a strap," and "I only take a fast bite for lunch." [22] Thomas Pynchon in *V.* soberly tells us about employment in the sewers of New York City, where there are wild disoriented hunts daily for alligators that have grown from the pet reptiles that were flushed down the toilet by urban children.

Any irreverent gesture toward the sanctified and the sancti-
monious risks ostracism, for such is the fate of all who would
parody the status quo. Black Humor often works to control such
potential disaffection, one especially acute in a fiction where the
protagonist is simultaneously an embodiment, and a disaffected
member, of society, through the device of the first-person narrator through which the space we inhabit is suddenly part of the
space that the narrator also occupies. As a result of this angle
of narration, we are drawn into his environment and merged with
his point of view. But the "inside" point of view (as Wayne Booth
calls it) creates for the author as serious a narrative problem as
it solves; for not only is the world depicted from the idiosyncratic
stance of an outsider perverse but it is also necessarily limited and
incomplete. For, unless the narrator's vision is identical to the
author's, the narrator's world must be a restricted one. Such a
limited sensibility militates against the inclusiveness, irony, and
impurity that is central to Black Humor's posit of a disorderly,
infinitely Protean universe. Hence, writers of Black Humor have
had to devise fictional forms that are enormously self-conscious;
they must be aware not only of their position but of the endless
other possible orbits that stand in relation to them. Their aim,
to use the words of Richard Kostelanetz in reference to Thomas
Pynchon,[23] is to formulate symbols for a metaphysical reality that
suggests not ambiguity but unbounded multiplicity.

In this respect, Robert Buckeye's recent admirable attempt in
"The Anatomy of the Psychic Novel" to distinguish among the
many practitioners of Black Humor is not as useful as it initially
promises to be. He argues that the "psychic" novel as written by
Günter Grass, Nabokov, Pynchon, Heller, and Hawkes is basically
multiple and uncertain; its subject, the incomplete and unful-
filled; its aim, the creation and preservation of psychic identity
"in face of history which renders events and actions meaningless
as well as science and technology which reduce man to mechanical and operational, biological and behavioral." This novel differs
from the novels of Bruce Jay Friedman and Terry Southern in its
consciousness "of the limitations of language in a world increasingly Orwellian." [24] Here, I think, Buckeye wanders from the
high road and stumbles in the dark into a culvert: that these
"psychic" authors might despairingly submit to the intrinsic limitations of language as a vehicle of knowledge is itself suspect,

when we remember with what verve and ingenuity Grass, Nabokov, Pynchon, and Hawkes, in particular, tyrannize over words. The *O altitudo* of Ebenezer Cooke, Barth's poet-laureate of Maryland, over a line of verse of his making, would surely gain their assent:

> "Sweet land!" he exclaimed. "Pregnant with song! Thy deliverer approacheth!"
> There was a conceit worth saving, he reflected: such subtle vistas of meaning in the word *deliverer*, for instance, with its twin suggestions of midwife and savior! (*The Sot-Weed Factor,* Chap. 11)

Differences there certainly are among the many kinds of Black Humor novels being written today, and Buckeye's effort at discrimination is salutary; but, in his concentration on presumed verbal limitations, he overlooks the more basic experiential limitations of a disorderly universe that inform the vision of these writers. For if—as our century's assumption of the absurd posits— we live in a world without visible cause and effect, where even comprehensive little packets of time and space no longer comfortably orient us, we remain undefined experientially. We exist in unrelatedness, like the inhabitants of Heaven whom Vonnegut depicts in Eliot Rosewater's unfinished novel as lamenting that "There is no inside here. There is no outside here. To pass through the gates in either direction is to go from nowhere to nowhere and from everywhere to everywhere" (*God Bless You, Mr. Rosewater,* Chap. 7). Restriction then, not in the ordinary sense but in its contrary guise of boundlessness, poses for these writers a major problem: How to cope with endless multiplicity? How to order and orient experience, without denying its inherent disorientation? This central question clearly affects the esthetic strategies of Black Humor.

At least six kinds of deployment are used to suggest the self-conscious awareness that the world of our sensibility impinges upon, and is invaded in turn by, the worlds of other sensibilities.

(1) The careful Jamesian distinction between narrator and author is blurred, allowing for the introduction of authorial responses to the narrator's vision that are not verified by the experience of the narrative. Both Céline and Nabokov adopt this maneuver in the conclusions of *Journey to the End of the Night*

and *Lolita*, respectively. A startling variation is the homogenizing, as Barth terms it,[25] of first and third person in some of Donleavy's and Nabokov's work.

(2) Corollary to the narratorial blur is the felt presence of the author throughout the novel. Nabokov employs this tactic in *Lolita* with the skill of a master chess player. He plants clues, introduces his own signature of the passionate pursuit of lepidoptery, and arbitrarily alters Humbert's physical appearance— all as a reminder to the reader that the omniscient control of the author is never in doubt.

(3) The human sense of time and the distinctions of history are blurred, until the present becomes a parodic reconstruction of the past, a compendium of all the human exercises in abstraction designed to impose connectiveness on the intervals of time. Barth and Pynchon are the most inventive practitioners of this ardent "betrayal" of experience.

(4) Literary parody offers these writers another dimension of self-consciousness to disclose how our verbal constructs are subjective perceptions of reality. The parodies of Nabokov, Barth, Pynchon, and Terry Southern, for example, comically remind us that other worlds, other patterns of reality, exist concurrently with those of our making. Their multidimensional presentations of human experience correct the tragic tendency (for instance, Herbert Stencil's and Humbert Humbert's errors) to mistake the reflection of the mind for a true record of the thing itself. Epistemologically, they represent efforts, in the phrase of Alfred Appel, "to exhaust the 'fictional gestures'" which would reduce the ineffable and diverse qualities of human experience to a convention of language.[26]

(5) The revered Aristotelian dogma of plot, while not completely ignored is obscured by a broadening of the independent role of incidents and surface details. The usual functional connection between plot and theme is blurred to permit apparently irrelevant incidents to develop bifocally in concurrence with the plot a related but more inconclusive vision of life. Friedman, along with Céline and Heller and Vonnegut whom he admires, generally employs this tactic in his novels.

(6) Activities and thoughts appear in these authors' negative aspects, expanding our sensibilities, like Alice through the Looking Glass, with a hint of "New thresholds, new anatomies." Thus

is suggested to our consciousness the suspicion that the arrangement of experience into either-or equations falsifies by delimitation the alternative infinites of *and* and *and*. Heller and Vonnegut frequently conceive of actions and events in such terms.

In neither Friedman's *Stern* nor his *A Mother's Kisses* does the symbolic action of the narrative give us the full statement of theme. Thus, while the plot of *Stern* deals with a Jewish protagonist's effort to avenge an insult to his wife, the novel is thematically much more ambitious than the subject of anti-Semitism; it casts a much wider net not only in its references to Stern's fantasies of sexual and social violence but also in those to the larger social arena in which these random acts purportedly occur. In short, while the plot obviously develops the theme, it does not encompass the whole of the thematic statement that the novel makes; therefore, plot and theme are not always in focus. Facts and incidents contribute to the theme, but their connection to the plot is tenuous. The soft, truncated, mechanized, and demented individuals Stern encounters at the rest home where he goes to cure an ulcer advance the plot little; but they dramatize the theme in great detail. Similarly, Stern's sexual adventure with the Puerto Rican girl, who looks like a battered caricature of Gene Tierney, says much about the nature of his sexual problem but very little directly about his fear of "the kike man" who had abused his wife.

Friedman has indicated in conversation that he deliberately strives for offhandedness: he wants an art that hides its design. To achieve this effect of artlessness, he will "throw away" his climaxes and bury his critical lines in a mass of surface objects.[27] The increased structural looseness of *A Mother's Kisses*, in comparison to *Stern*, represents, therefore, a conscious artistic choice. The plot—Joseph's effort to get into a college during the crowded post-war years—at least approaches, even if fuzzily and hesitantly, the theme of his Oedipal relationship with his mother Meg; but Friedman refuses to do more than circle warily and tangentially about the real theme of the novel: the sexual (and emotional) education of a boy in the accelerated pluralism of post-World-War-II America. Joseph's contretemps with a Viennese girl at summer camp, his exploratory *rapprochement* with the co-eds at a neighboring college in Kansas, his night-long vigils to catch glimpses of his sister undressing, his furtive peeks at the half

disclosed torso of his mother's Irish crony, his contribution to
the gang bathtub bathing of a neighborhood girl—all have next
to nothing to do with the resolution of the plot but are at the
very center of the novel's statement about Joseph's growing pains.

A similar loosening of plot also occurs in other ways. In
Stern the controlling metaphor of buttocks works to diffuse plot
and theme by commenting ironically on the hero's timidity (his
lack of *sternness*) and by alluding not only to his wide-hipped
womanish appearance but also to his latent bisexuality. In *A
Mother's Kisses,* the controlling metaphor of Meg's minty mouth
pretty much bypasses the plot to emphasize the theme. To in-
crease this diffusion, Friedman also tags minor characters with
strong secondary metaphors—the thundering thighs of the summer camp director Salamandro and the Bates basketball player,
the château milieu of the French girl, the middle-aged manu-
facturers' faces of the fourteen-year-old camp waiters—that function independently of the central controlling image.

In the apparent surface chaos of Friedman's novels—in his almost frantic desire to unwind the skein of experience to the bare
spool—we have what John Barth (in reference specifically to
Jorge Luis Borges) has considered to be contemporary literature's
baroque exhaustion of the frightening guises of reality.[28] This
Regressus in infinitum, or endless recounting of appearances, is
a logical outgrowth of the world posited in Black Humor writing.
As one of its anthologists has remarked, "There are no certainties
in Black Humor," [29] just as there is none in the world it chron-
icles. The warrant officer sick with malaria in Heller's *Catch-22*
voices the central vision of Black Humor when he remarks to
Yossarian that

> "There just doesn't seem to be any logic to this system of re-
> wards and punishment. Look what happened to me. If I had
> gotten syphillis or a dose of clap for my five minutes of passion
> on the beach instead of this damned mosquito bite, I could see
> some justice. But malaria? *Malaria?* Who can explain malaria as
> a consequence of fornication? . . . Just for once I'd like to see all
> these things sort of straightened out, with each person getting
> exactly what he deserves. It might give me some confidence in
> this universe." (Chap. 17)

Not just the warrant officer's words but also the setting for his statement, the base hospital, provide Black Humor with what is practically a literary convention. Borges' vision of human experience as a labyrinth is a nearly perfect metaphysical conceit for Black Humor's world picture. Another almost equally appropriate is undiagnosed illness: Yossarian's puzzling liver condition, Eliot Rosewater's amnesia, Sebastian Dangerfield's debilitating malaises, Cabot Wright's blackouts, Jacob Horner's and Ebenezer Cooke's recurrent immobilities, Stern's ulcer, Joseph's father's mysterious back ailment, and Meg's periodic sieges of sitting around in a bathrobe. Friedman's novels, particularly, abound in enigmatic balloonings of arm and head, in inexplicable lapses and convalescences. While recovering from an attack of swelling, Joseph expresses surprise that anything sick ever heals: "One day, he felt, it would be announced that the whole germ theory of disease was a hoax, that there was no such thing as a germ . . . that all medicines were silly, doctors could learn all they needed to know in two weeks of school and that when people got better it was a wild coincidence" (*Kisses*, 126). Implicit in Joseph's expectations is a denial of the meaningful relatedness of actions on which the accepted empirical notions of the physical world are posited.

If causal sequence *(non sequitur)* and temporal sequence *(post hoc; ergo, propter hoc)* are questioned, then technically all history may be a sham—as Barth and Pynchon have been pointing out delightedly at great length. Without a logic of events to narrow the possibilities of an action to one or several consequences, a Pandora's box of possibilities is uncapped. At a signal from the leader of an overcoated gang after he had distributed bars of halvah, a girl may undress "as though she always disrobed after halvah servings" (*Kisses*, 186). If her nudity follows such illogical directives, why could it not just as easily be triggered by an afternoon on the ski slopes, or a snappy speech by the vice-president, or an hour of television cartoons? Suddenly, a simple letter of the alphabet like *V* contains myriad identities behind its bland mask, through its intrinsic capacity of combination with other letters to allude mysteriously to illimitable persons and places.

To an individual assailed by an infinite number of possibilities of action, the terror of daily life with its mandatory decisions axiomatically waxes out of all proportion to the situation. Hence an assemblage of the familiar, as in much Pop art, becomes a strategy for encroachment on the unknown. In this light, the structural peculiarities of some other well-known Black Humor novels, which have attracted critical attention on that account, become explicable: the compulsive return again and again to the same action in Heller's *Catch-22*; the inexhaustible guises and disguises in Barth's *The Sot-Weed Factor*; the transformations of places and persons, with the same initial letter in Pynchon's *V.*; and the endless refractions of mirror words and images, puns, parodies, and doubles in Nabokov's *Lolita*.

Even more to the point is the shift from refined selectivity to omnibus appetite for experience in so many of these novels. "Through being thrown out of every place," Céline has Bardamu console himself in *Journey to the End of the Night*, "you'll surely finish up by finding out what it is that frightens all these bloody people so" (218–19). Hence his tireless journeying to face the terror of war, the horror of colonial Africa, the hysteria of industrial America, and the nausea of the slums of Paris. This quest collapses together centuries of events in Barth's and Pynchon's novels, and it links earth with intergalactic space in Vonnegut's novels. In both Vonnegut's *Sirens of Titan* and his *Cat's Cradle* the joke on man is that he may comb through all the debris of this world and still not learn toward what end his life has moved, for the purposefulness of terrestrial actions may be tied to extrahuman cosmic ends. What preoccupies these authors is not desire for experience itself so much as a need to find, in Ebenezer Cooke's words, an Ariadne's thread marking our "path through the labyrinth of Life" (Chap. 3)—a need to cajole out of experience all its variations, as a way of getting at the causes of reality, of connecting us with our starting place. Like Menelaus on the shores of Pharos in Euripedes' play, exhorting direction from the Proteus of life,[30] these authors are less bent on judging the multiple appearances of reality than on simply knowing them —as the only desperate way left to wring from experience a modicum of sanity, perhaps of salvation.

In a limited sense, then, Robert Scholes is right in noting the interest of the Black Humorists with construction; but he minimizes their seriousness when he characterizes this concern as playful or artful. Like the painterly and post-painterly movements of abstract expressionism, hard edge, and pop art, the

Black Humorist's intensive search through form for the springs of twentieth-century existence is worthy of our attention. If he cannot be numbered among those moral activists who change the visible face of things, the Black Humorist is, nevertheless, in his passionate concentration on the hallucinations of reality, as Knickerbocker insists, one of the "keepers of conscience." [31] Among the writers of contemporary fiction, the Black Humorist is conspicuously risking the resources of the imagination to find new modes of order for the raw materials of experience. One of today's adventurers into the murky corners of the human mind and the social soul, his vision is as necessary to individual health as the discovery of the Salk vaccine; for the Black Humorist is working a revolution in our sensibilities, and he is instructing us anew in ways of perceiving reality.

CHAPTER *2*

Stern

B LACK HUMOR is as much a product of the postwar technological society as is smog, congested freeways, supersonic
airplanes, and the flight to the suburbs. It has moved beyond the
personal dilemma of the individual as formulated by postwar existentialism, which defined man metaphysically silhouetted
against the backdrop of an indifferent natural universe. Black
Humor impatiently shrugs aside such philosophical contexts, for
it is profoundly distrustful of system making. Without abating
one jot the intrinsic isolation of man, Black Humor turns its attention primarily to the social and historical contradictions of
his world.

Friedman, like his fellow writers of the Black Humor persua-
sion, is concerned ostensibly with what might almost be considered, if they were not so immediate and real, the clichés of
modern culture: the false values that have barnacle-like encrusted
our daily actions until their original meaning has been lost to
sight. In concentrating our attention on the act again, the Black
Humorist is performing a service not unlike those painters and
sculptors bent on renewing our awareness of the found object—
of the common, prosaic things-in-themselves of a technological
civilization. The workaday commuter, the inane casual conversation, the perilous neighborhood drugstore, Momism, anti-Semitism, suburbia, sex, ulcers, the hidden traps in house buying, the
subversive quiet of street corners, the super sexuality of Negroes,
crowded universities, old age, inept craftsmanship—all undergo
the scrutiny of Friedman's saturnine gaze.

But Friedman is preoccupied with more than the surfaces of the
"found objects" of urban existence. Of the characteristics of Black
Humor reviewed in Chapter 1, the savage divisiveness of individuals in our society receives his most intense attention. His recurrent theme is the threat to being that informs contemporary life.

Incipient in many of our actions is the felt tremor of a civil terror. Violence is a national heritage of frontier America, as well as an earmark of this century of racial extermination and two world wars. It leads a subconscious existence in "the dream life of the nation," as Norman Mailer remarks in *The Presidential Papers.* In our psychic lives there is "a subterranean river of untapped, ferocious, lonely and romantic desires"[1] that pose a constant threat to the smooth routine of our mundane affairs. This menace that lurks beneath the surface of the bland and the ordinary informs the pages of all Friedman's fiction, but especially those of his first novel *Stern.*

Acclaimed for its mature grasp of twentieth-century neuroses and for its nervous, energetic style,[2] the novel has for its hero the frightened, harried Stern. The irony of his name is indicative of the bittersweet attitude that the novel adopts toward human failings and personal inadequacies. In effect, Friedman finds only the comic gesture appropriate for dealing with life in this century; for an electronics culture is too faceless to elicit the tragic impulse. Only the transcendent safety valve of laughter adequately refracts the monolithic facade of contemporary existence into recognizable—and endurable—human feelings again. Consequently, the novel demands from the reader an ambivalent response toward Stern who is characterized simultaneously as a humorous victim of society's follies and as an inept, despicable object of ridicule. We both sympathize with his hesitant longings for human contact and are repulsed by his spineless, self-centered obsessions.

I *Stern*

Stern is a "tall, soft man" (20) with spreading thighs.[3] He is married to a "fragrant, long-nosed" woman (10) who had avidly slept with him at college and then lured him into marriage after a year of separation by threatening to elope with a Venezuelan. When she put her head deep into his lap and said, "I've been so lousy bad," Stern "knew he was bound to her for a hundred years" (42). A mild, anxious man, who is as prone to fantasies as Walter Mitty—but in which he plays the victim more often than the hero—Stern is one of the faceless millions who reliably hold undistinguished jobs (he writes copy for labels) and who adequately provide for wife and child.

Although Friedman is not writing in the mode of such current Jewish-American novelists as Saul Bellow and Bernard Malamud, his conception of Stern does reflect a vogue for the luckless figure of the *shlimazel* as hero. When Stern tries several joyous push-ups in a wooded glade on the way to work, exuberant at the beauty of the morning, he inevitably rises with manure on his hands. He is, however, less saintly than Isaac Bashevis Singer's Gimpel the Fool; and he is less innocent than Sholem Aleichem's Tevye the Dairyman. Stern's background is the gray anonymity of the lower-middle-class urban Jew; and Friedman sketches with great economy a Jewish family of petty mercantilistic background (a rich aunt owns a hardware store). After the final prayers of the annual Seder on the first night of Passover, this aunt always turns on the lights in the store to let each of the Sedergoers put in a large order, which she lets him have at cost. There are three uncles who carry on internecine warfare during the Passover but enjoy a long armistice the rest of the year. There is a dotty grandmother "of indeterminate age" who buries bits of food around the apartment and who spends most of her day praying, "bowing and singing softly and wetting the pages of her prayer book as she slapped them along" (60).

Stern's father is a "small, round-shouldered" (56), silent man, who has eked out a drab three-room-apartment existence for his wife and two children as a cutter of shoulder pads. He is a man whose inner life is occupied with the minutiae of the daily routine. Stern remembers having his hand slapped as a boy when he cut from the new side of a quarter-pound stick of butter that had been started on the other side, and his father's instructing him profoundly, "That's no way to do it. I can't understand you" (103). Now, when Stern meets his father for dinner in the city, the conversation is restricted to the machinery of the meeting. "How long have you been waiting?" he greets Stern. "I thought I'd take a crosstown bus, get myself a transfer, and then walk the extra two blocks over to Sixth. If I'd known you were going to be early, I'd have come all the way up by subway and the hell with the walking. How'd you get up here?" Later, during the meal, he asks Stern, "How do you plan on getting back? I think, in your situation, your best bet is to walk over west and catch a bus going downtown. Lets you off slightly north of the station. You can duck down and walk the rest of the way underground or, if you like, you can grab a cab. I haven't figured out how I'm going home myself. . . ." (184).

Stern's relationship with his mother is more intense. She had been a "tall, voluptuous woman," with ambitions of owning a house in Florida and of decorating it in Chinese modern. Her husband's mild nature, however, had aged her and driven her to drink; now, she clings furiously to her faded youth. She encases her "slack antique thighs" (105) in toreador pants; rinses her hair in henna; executes little dance steps in subways, in bars, on the street; and loudly insists in restaurants and other public places that her decaying charms "could make" this or that strange young man "in ten seconds" (105). In a few deft strokes, Friedman portrays with obvious fondness a recognizable literary type—the loud, brassy matron. Instead of playing her for laughs as an odious or ridiculous figure, however, he transforms her into a lovable comic individual, whose zany brashness—she blithely hails cars on the street instead of cabs—wins our affection and admiration. She is a Jewish heir of Falstaff's outrageousness and Don Quixote's audaciousness.

Clearly, Friedman's vision tends to be comic rather than satirical; tender, rather than sharp. Whatever tendency he may have toward Jewish sentimentality is rigorously qualified by the Black Humor tilt of the contemporary situation in which he places his characters. As a boy, Stern had a mild Oedipus relationship with his mother. He always accompanied her to a mountain resort in the summer, where he was the only boy among a bevy of young women. Here he was introduced to a preview of sex by way of nervous showers with his mother and panty glimpses on the volleyball court. He would lie in the bottom of a boat while "his great-breasted mother, wearing a polka-dotted bathing suit that stared at him like a thousand nipples," rowed over to the hut of a forest ranger. Afterward, his mother would say to him, "A hundred girls at the hotel and I'm the only one can make him" (130); and Stern, in anguish and with a sense of loss, would try not to think of "his dated mother . . . doing old-fashioned things with strange, dull men" (105). Despite all the flaunting of bodies, Stern had to learn incredulously from a busboy in back of the resort kitchen about the "actual machinery" of the sex act.

Understandably, Stern's fantasies are often sexual: he imagines himself to be unencumbered by ineffectuality and clumsiness and to be a Jewish Don Juan loose in the bedrooms of New York suburbia. But his sexual inadequacies with his wife, contrariwise, cloud these daydreams with nagging suspicions that he may be a cuckold in his own house. The sight of her kissing José, a modern dance instructor, who has brought her home from a lesson, lights his fears like a roman candle. The tight jumper she wears snugly over flaring thighs, with the crease of her underwear showing through, causes him to wonder suddenly if "she had just thrown on her clothes in a great hurry." "I saw a kiss," he says accusingly. As a stomach-sinking afterthought, he adds, "I saw tongues." "No, you didn't," she answers. "I can't help what *he* did. I didn't use my tongue." "Oh my God, *then there was a tongue*" (109), Stern moans in consternation.

These two parts of Stern's life—his Jewishness and his sexual fears—provide the substance of the narrative. In a moment of daring indiscretion, he had moved his wife and child out of the safe familiarity of their New York City apartment and into the Gentile strangeness of suburbia. There, isolated, among unfriendly neighbors who will not let their children play with Jews, Stern's wife is shoved by a brawny man, falls in the gutter, and displays herself to him (she wears nothing underneath her skirt). Apprised of the incident, Stern feels the masculine need to avenge the insult inflicted upon her; but he worries even more about the "kike man's" heavy Italian arms and about the army of Italian relatives. He develops an ulcer—a great hot brocade of pain in his middle—which happily releases him from the nagging obligation to act in defense of his wife and sends him, instead, to a rest home for five weeks.

But he finds nothing changed upon his return home. His little boy is still picked on and called "Matzoh" by the other children. The "kike man" still occupies the house down the road and continues to darken Stern's every waking moment. His wife's attendance of dancing classes continues to terrorize him with fantasies of her infidelity with the dancing master. The morning of his departure for the rest home, he had made love to his wife "as though to nail her down, to stake her in some way so there would be no smoothly coordinated backseat tumbles with José during his absence." "He went at her with a frenzy, as though by the sheer force of his connection he could do something to her that would keep her quiet and safe and chaste for two weeks." But Stern is inadequate to her needs: "when he fell to the side he saw with panic that she was unchanged, unmarked, her skin still cold and unrelieved" (110–11). When he observes his wife after the weeks of his absence, she is dressed in a low-cut, loose-fitting blouse that reveals the start of her nipples; and his old terrors begin:

> Stern wondered whether she had gone to bed with the [dance] instructor, getting into tangled, modern dance positions with him. How did he know she hadn't spent the entire five weeks of his sickness at endless, exhausting, intricately choreographed love-making, flying to the instructor seconds after she had deposited Stern at the Home? She seemed curled up, contented, shimmering with peace, as though someone had finally pressed the right buttons and relieved the dry, chattering hunger Stern had never been able to cope with. Perhaps she had gone to him in a desperate way, knowing that the instructor, however thin of bone and feminine of gesture, would never allow her to be insulted and would attack any offender with Latin fury. In any case, the secret was locked between her warm thighs. He would never know what had gone on, and he felt a drooping, weakened sensation. . . . (161–62)

The ulcer gives way to a nervous breakdown. It is ironical that neither Stern's throbbing duodenal tract nor his trembling nervous system proves to be excessive or serious. In five weeks of rest his stomach calms down. In little more time his nerves stop jumping. "I had the mildest nervous breakdown in town," he tells someone in the office. "I didn't miss a day of work" (181). As Stern lugubriously states, he suffers from "the least romantic disease of all" (146). A mediocre, little *Massenmensch,* he is afflicted with the ailments of a modern mass society. Appropriately, he is not allowed the heroics of a dangerous illness.

After weeks of choking and trembling, of retiring desperate with perspiration to the safety of his bed, he calms down abruptly. One evening he discovers his wife's Polish cleaning woman on her knees in the broom closet. His wife had gone to the movies, so he talked for two hours to this "small, pinched wrinkle of a woman," who seemed to have been made from "a compound of flowered discount dresses, cleaning fluid, and lean

Polish winters" (181). Her disjointed fragments of advice—"You got to just . . . sooner or later . . . I mean if a man don't . . . This old world going to . . . When a fully grown man . . ."—inexplicably soothe him. A few nights later he rises on an impulse from the dinner table, walks down the road to the "kike man's" house, and calls him out for a fight.

Even in the act of righting the insult to his wife, Stern is not allowed the luxury of heroics. The fight is a farce. Filled with fright, thinking that he should have brought along "an observer to run for an intern," Stern meekly follows the man to the back-yard where he receives "a great freezing kiss" of a blow on the ear. His one punch in return is "girlish and ineffectual." As if it were he who had delivered the punch in the ear, Stern says, "Don't talk that way to someone's wife and push her." The "kike man" proves unreconstructive. When he snears that he "won't," Stern lamely replies, "You better not." His ear leaking blood, Stern turns and walks home, "shaking with fear of the man all over again." He follows his wife upstairs to their son's bedroom; there, kneeling quietly, he holds both "a fraction longer than he'd intended." His protective hug, initiated by his desire "to try something a little theatrical," has become a plea for comfort and protection (189–91).

II Stern and Society

Stern's fears are the special ones of the Jew living in a White-Anglo-Saxon-Protestant community. But the reader does not have to nudge the language very hard to recognize in his anxieties the terrors of ineffectuality felt by man in the twentieth century. Like so many ordinary citizens today, who acquiesce to illegality and to crime because they do not wish to get involved with the law, Stern regards the police as potential enemies, not as upholders of law and order. Afraid to call them to protect him against his neighbors, he pictures them as "large, neutral-faced men with rimless glasses who would accuse him of being a newcomer making vague troublemaking charges" (30). He is suspicious of justice meted out by commissioners and judges; and he worries about offending the local firemen, fearful that they might turn "deliberately sluggish" and let his house burn to the ground, while playing "weak water jets on the roof, far short of the mark" (25).

Ironically, the conformist in this century finds his chief source of apprehension in those same institutions that he turns to for succor. By limiting himself to their bureaucratic order, he hopes to impose a rationale upon his existence. Instead, he finds himself paralyzingly isolated, bereft of individuality, a faceless integer who counts simply as a population statistic. If he happens to be like Stern, he fails to convince even his wife that he is a person distinguishable from other human beings. When they go to their second-floor bedroom, she has him go first because she does not "like to go upstairs in front of *people*" (191; my italics).

Underlying Stern's obsession with the "kike man's" hostility is clearly the larger question of his place in society. Stern is afflicted not only with an ulcer but also with the more psychically virulent American malady of wanting to be liked—of wanting to be accepted as a full-fledged, paid-up member of a group. When he checks out of the rest home, he feels "as though by getting healthy he had violated a rotted, fading charter" of the other, sicker inmates: "He had come into their sick club under false pretenses, enjoying the decayed rituals, and all the while his body wasn't ruined at all. He was secretly healthy, masquerading as a shattered man so that he could milk the benefits of their crumbling society. And now he felt bad about not being torn up as they were" (158).

As with the Waverley hero in Sir Walter Scott's novels, not differentness but sameness is Stern's social goal. In the novel, he realizes this ambition only once, on the night he "does the town" with a local girl and two other inmates of the rest home; and his reaction to their togetherness indicates its prime importance for his psychic well-being. They have a fracas in a bar and leave hurriedly before the police arrive. As they jog down the street, Stern thinks happily that "they were comrades of a sort and he was glad to be with them, to be doing things with them, to be running and bellowing to the sky at their sides; he was glad their lives were tangled up together. It was so much better than being a lone Jew stranded on a far-off street, your exit blocked by a heavy-armed kike hater in a veteran's jacket" (149).

So urgent is Stern's desire for communal acceptance that it takes precedence over his need to compensate for sexual inferiorities. Even though he makes love to the Puerto Rican girl and is excited to try it again, he joins forces with the other two boys

when they begin to toss her into the air straddled on a broom-
stick. "Ooh, you really hurt me . . . you cruddy bastards," she
cries.

> Stern felt good that she had addressed all three of them, not
> excluding him, and it thrilled him to be flying out of her apart-
> ment with his new friends, all three howling and smacking each
> other with laughter at the pole episode. He wanted to be with
> them, not with her. He needed buddies, not a terrible Puerto
> Rican girl. He needed close friends to stand around a piano
> with and sing the Whiffenpoof song, arms around each other,
> perhaps before shipping out somewhere to war. If his dad got
> sick, he needed friends to stand in hospital corridors with him
> and grip his arm. He needed guys to stand back to back with
> him in bars and take on drunks. These were tattered, broken
> boys, one in a wheelchair, but they were buddies. (156)

A man's sense of identity depends in part on his relationship
to the age-groups of his society. Friedman captures the peculiar
nonexistence of today's Everyman, trapped in an impersonal
round of homogenized activities, by portraying him as an American Jew who is alienated from Judaic values but as yet un-
assimilated by American traditions. Thus Stern belongs, at least in
this respect, in the company of the many Jewish fictional heroes
of the 1950's and 1960's. He shares with Bellow's protagonist the
disinheritance of the American Jew; but, at the same time, he
partakes of the dissociation of the Black Humor protagonist of
the 1960's. He is both physically part of and mentally apart from
the collective community. He lives in it but does not belong to
it. That he is a nonperson is vividly dramatized by his lack of
involvement with people. With neither wife, parents, co-worker,
employer, friend, nor acquaintances does he successfully com-
municate.

Stern is truly a man alone, despite his efforts at conformity. He
occupies space and generates emotional steam; but he remains
self-contained. Although he attended Hebrew School as prepara-
tion for the Bar Mitzvah ceremony at age thirteen conferring
adulthood on him, he was taught no great religious traditions by
his father. As a boy, he was taken to holiday services

where he stood in ignorance among bowing, groaning men who wore brilliantly embroidered shawls. Stern would do some bows and occasionally let fly a complicated imitative groan, but when he sounded out he was certain one of the old genuine groaners had spotted him and knew he was issuing a phony. Stern thought it was marvelous that the old men knew exactly when to bow and knew the groans and chants and melodies by heart. He wondered if he would ever get to be one of their number . . . even with three years of Hebrew School under his belt Stern still felt a loner among the chanting sufferers at synagogues. After a while he began to think you could never get to be one of the groaners through mere attendance at Hebrew School. You probably had to pick it all up in Europe. (54)

During the war, he, as "a nonflying officer in a flying service" (66), "yearned for Air Force comrades" (70). Once, flying as a passenger in a general's luxury B-17 and sitting alone in the bombardier's bubble, he felt that "he had been put in a special Jewish seat and sealed off from the camaraderies in the plane's center." As the plane circled a West Coast Air Force base, he had gotten airsick. He had "spread a thin layer of vomit around his bubble and then kneeled inside it as the plane landed, the pilots and other flying personnel filing by him in silence" (67).

Ostracism, real and fancied, follows him in civilian life wherever he goes. Riding to and from the embattled isolation of his suburban home, he sits amidst the easy fellowship of the commuter train, alone and worried about how he should act, fearful that he had already "violated his twentieth rule since the trip began" (100). When he tries to emulate the inane chatter of two commuters, he is frozen silent by a cold glare. At the rest home, his educated speech gets him immediately into trouble. "What did you say lovely for?" one of the patients asks him pettishly. "We're just a bunch of guys. The way I see it, you think maybe you're better than the rest of us" (123). And so ironically his thoughtless effort to be ingratiating—one key to the novel's conception of Stern as representative man—contributes to the concrete reality of loneliness in his life.

Stern is driven by the desire to *be* the modern American male. His move from the city to the suburbs, from a Jewish neighborhood to a Gentile community, gives warp to this pattern. Intimately linked to Stern's social impulse is a psychosexual crisis which goes far toward explaining the excessive importance that the insult of the "kike man" assumes for Stern.

III   *The Rites of Passage*

In its profoundest reaches, the novel is concerned with the rites of passage. Historically, the trauma of an American emergent into the nuclear and electronics age is a recurrent subject of Black Humor. Psychosocially, in our time, the American Jew has passed from the Eastern European *shtetl* to an American urban identity. Underlying both historical and specific post-World-War-II metamorphoses is the universal rite of initiation, of which puberty ceremonies are one instance. Psychosexually, each man passes from preadolescent identification with parents to adult independence and community power.

The conflicts in Stern are drawn sharply on both the psychosexual and the psychosocial levels. Stern wishes to be a big man, a powerful man, a "Big Jew"—that is, a Gentile. He wishes to be a member in good standing of the WASP Club of America. He wishes to be the persecuting "kike man," the real man; and his move to the Gentile suburbs is a vital step in his transformation. At the same time, Stern wishes masochistically to remain Jewish; like a mother-dominated boy, he desires to be feminine and persecuted, passively and guiltily suffering punishment as a sign of divine and maternal love. In any drastic alteration of identity, strong psychological tensions are bound to surface. With uncanny sensitivity to the ways that human conflict betrays itself in behavior, Friedman links Stern's social aspirations to ancient ethnic and psychic feelings: to the feminine abasement involved in the Hebrew people's glorification of a masculine deity, and to the profound bisexual ambivalences intrinsic to the coming of age of the individual.[4]

With these assumptions in mind, much of the novel that appears random and irrelevant assumes significance and pattern. Stern's obsession with the "kike man" reflects, in part, his desire to be like that big-armed, sexually aggressive, *goyish* or Gentile, Italian-American. Of importance is that when Stern exaggerates the presumed insult to his wife—who insists that "It doesn't make any difference" (13)—he stresses the "kike man's" sexual interest in her more than the man's anti-Semitism. The "very next night" after the "violation," he forces his wife to re-enact the scene. "Still in his overcoat," he "caught her wrists around the oven and said, 'I just want to see how it happened. . . . I want to get a picture in my mind of what it was all about. Get on the floor and show me exactly how you were. How your legs were when you were down there. It's important.'" When she objects, he grabs her with the brutal incisiveness of the "kike man" and throws her to the kitchen floor (47). With her jumper flying above her knees, she lies supine before him as she had the previous day before the man down the road, the man who plays an accepted role in the suburban community.

As a commanding, authoritative figure, the "kike man" appears to Stern to be devoted to the social, political, economic, and religious knowledge to which Stern aspires. His relationship to Stern, one might say, is that of the tribal elder to the initiate in a puberty rite. For Stern, the "kike man" (ironically, considering his Italian and Roman Catholic origins) represents the White-Anglo-Saxon-Protestant ideal, the warrior who sports a "veteran's organization jacket" (52) and displays "giant American flags flying thrillingly and patriotically from . . . every window" (74). Like most of Western civilization, Stern equates militant courage historically with the Aryan and cowardly passivity with the Jew. Hence he remembers his own wartime experience in the Air Force with shame: he "connected his nonflying status with his Jewishness, as though flying were a golden, crew-cut, gentile thing" (66). On the other hand, "Jewish boys did accounting" and "administrative Air Force things" (67–68).

Longing to identify with the Anglo-Saxon Americans, Stern remembers the night he was mistaken for a flier by a civilian flying instructor who had trained Israeli pilots during the Arab-Israeli war: a "husky . . . man with much blond hair curled romantically down over his forehead." "You Jews fly well, Big Jew," the romantic gentleman had intoned at Stern; "Big Jew, you fly a deadly plane." Thrilling to the unaccustomed acclaim, Stern thought:

> He saw me as the strong and quiet Jew in a brigade of inter-national fighters. I might have been the Big Swede or the Big Prussian, but I was the Big Jew, the quiet, silent one with bitter memories and a past of mystery, a man you could count on to

slip silently through enemy lines and slit a throat, the one with
skills at demolition who could blow a bridge a thousand ways,
brilliant at weaponry, a quiet man with strong and magic hands
who could open any safe and fix an exhausted aircraft, fly it, too,
if necessary. "Send the Big Jew. He knows how to kill. He'll get
through. He says little, but no one kills a man better, and it
is said that when a woman has been to bed with him she will
never be loved better as long as she lives." (73–74)

This last thought points to another false assumption about
Jews that afflicts Stern with self-doubts: he accepts the notion
that effeminacy is at the basis of the Jew's unwarlike habits. The
controlling metaphor of buttocks insistently defines this belief.
Stern has fat, womanish hips; and he is sensitive of them. He
would like to say to the "man who'd kiked his wife and peered
between her legs": " 'You've got me wrong. I'm no kike. Come
and see my empty house. My bank account is lean. I drive an old
car, too, and Cousy thrills me at the backcourt just as you. No
synagogue has seen me in ten years. *It's true my hips are wide,
but I have a plan for thinness. I'm no kike.'* " (my italics, 74).

As an adjunct to physical valor, then, Stern sees athletic prowess and sexual virility as hallmarks of Anglo-Saxondom. Whereas
he is unable to cope with "the dry, chattering [sexual] hunger"
of his wife (162), he imagines the "kike man" to be a potent
conqueror capable of stabbing her sexually and getting her "to
wriggle and whimper with enjoyment" (94). In this contest, we
see the importance to Stern of the encounter with the Puerto
Rican girlfriend of the two "toughest" Gentiles at the Grove
Rest Home: to complete the reversal of roles, the two masculine
inmates sit under the lady's hairdryers, in impotent acquiescence,
while Stern "seduces" their female companion. With that act he
becomes the aggressive "kike man" who violates another's
woman; he is the forceful American conquering a despised inferior race.

In short, there is a real sense in which Stern's response to life
partakes of the "kike man's" anti-Semitism. At college, he and his
Jewish boardinghouse friends had self-consciously satirized their
Jewishness and had paid scant attention to Jewish girls in their
avid pursuit of "the gentile queens" (64). It is an easy step from
the self-hatred of his college days to his present mawkish desire
to assuage the malice of the "kike man" with assurances that

"Jews did not sit all day in mysterious temples"; instead, they, like other Americans, "played baseball and, despite a tendency to short-windedness, had good throwing arms" (141).

Stern, however, is unable—and unwilling—to divest himself fully of his Jewish origins. The ambiguous sentiment behind the words he and his college friends used to substitute for the real lyrics of popular songs epitomizes the duality of his response to a change of identity. "I'm glad I met you, you wonderful you" emerged as "I'm glad you're Jewish, you wonderful Jew" (63). The mixture of pride and self-loathing in such transfigurations informs Stern's image of himself as an American. When he went to college in Oregon, he told people, "I don't care much about being a Jew. There's only one thing: each year I like to go and hear the Shofar blown on Rosh Hashanah. It sort of ties the years together for me." The alienation is apparent here, but the bravado of the words also contains a desperate reluctance to let go of his buried Jewish life. It is as though standing outside synagogues each year and listening to the ancient sound of the ram's horn is a "concession to his early Jewish days," which would somehow keep Stern "just the tiniest bit Jewish, in case it turned out some- day that a scorecard really was kept on people" (61–62). Sim- ilarly, at Grove's Rest Home, he rebuffs Feldner the Jew so that he might impress his Gentile friends with his skill at playing base- ball, only to regret immediately his curtness and to want to shout to Feldner, "Come back. You're more to me than these blond fellows" (141).

Stern's effort to be an American suburbanite is obviously full of psychic, as well as social, peril for him. Friedman gives full emotional expression to the trauma of being socially born anew, of becoming another person, by recognizing its similarity to the sexual ambivalences endemic to emergent manhood. Stern's hesi- tancy to pass over wholly into American life is echoed in his infantilism. His son is a blanket sucker; and Stern, horrified by his family's suburban isolation, "had a picture of all three of them, his wife, his son, himself, sitting on the lawn, sucking blankets, shaking and trying to rock themselves to sleep" (38). His reluc- tance to progress emotionally beyond childhood dependence to adult responsibility is expressive of the distaff half of a bisexuality residual in boyhood, which has traditionally been exorcised in puberty rites. The almost pathogenic-like parallel of such Oedipal

behavior to that elicited by Judaism adds resonance to the already compromised impulses of Stern's gesture at passage.

Stern's subconscious sexual problem—his submission to a bru-
tally seductive mother and the fearful "gaping blackness between
her legs" (130), as well as his contempt for a passive father,
which completes the psychological picture—most fully reflects the
pertinacity of his Jewishness. The demon mother, or female
castrator, beginning with Lilith, has obsessed the human mind;
and it left a permanent mark on Judaism during the agonizing
shift of the early Hebrews from primeval mother Goddess cults
to patriarchal monotheism.[5] Fearful of her phallic power, ortho-
dox Judaism rendered the woman sexually unexciting; her head
was shaved; she wore a wig and long sleeves; man was warned
to avoid her eyes and her voice, and to prefer instead a passive,
scholarly tie with the father-God, a liaison abetted by the Jewish
renunciation of physical violence and aggression in general.

This masculine role of submissiveness was also strengthened by
the special bond between God and Israel, which was one of
punishment inflicted by an all powerful deity on His chosen as a
way of His ensuring their love of Him. Suffering was interpreted
as a purification and as a sign of God's love as much as of His
chastisement for past sin. Masochism glorified as a virtue appears already in the later Jewish prophets. The subsequent history of the Jews—their two thousand years' endurance of rapine
and outrage at the hands of other nations—has, according to most
psychoanalytic students of Judaism,[6] intensified the Oedipal
problem inherent in their religious practices. The Jew's psychology, Hannah Arendt has contended,[7] demands that he play
victim to a victimizer. If there is no tyrant, he invents one to
satisfy his spirit's need for subjugation and abasement.

This side of Stern's nature, attesting to its basic importance in
the total strategy of the novel, receives full symbolic development in the narrative. Stern is deeply divided in his response to
the "kike man." Not only does he wish to emulate the man's
presumed masculinity, but he also wishes to be the object of that
masculinity's desire. When his wife strenuously objects to her
re-enactment of the insult, Stern replies, "All right, then—me."
Lying on the kitchen floor and using his topcoat to simulate her
dress, he becomes his wife. He "drew the coat slightly above his
knees and said, 'This way?'" Three times at the negative nod of

his wife, he hitches the coat higher. Finally he "flung the overcoat back over his hips, his legs sprawling." At his wife's "yes," he said, " 'Jesus' and ran upstairs to sink in agony upon the bed. But he felt excited, too" (48).

The precise nature of Stern's sexual excitement becomes apparent when his ulcer [8] makes itself felt. He is warming tea at midnight in the kitchen, the setting of his re-enactment of the outrage, when "an electric shaft of pain charged through Stern's middle and flung him to the floor, his great behind slapping icily against the kitchen tile. It was as though the kike man's boot had stamped through Stern's mouth, plunging downward, elevator-swift, to lodge finally in his bowels, all the fragile and delicate things within him flung aside" (74). The brutal rape, the oral impregnation, implicit in the narration of the ulcer attack hardly needs explanation. After seeing a doctor to confirm his suspicions about his stomach, Stern informs his employer, Belavista, that he must go away for a while. In an effort to describe the ulcer, he says "You feel as though a baby with giant inflated cheeks is in there" (91); and Belavista promises Stern to continue his salary, as if addressing a valuable secretary in the family way.

As forlorn about his ulcer as an unwed girl with news of her pregnancy, Stern imagines transferring his ulcer into the belly of a woman by way of sexual intercourse with her (98). On the commuter train that evening, he suffers "morning sickness" and vomits (100–1). At home and in bed, he tries to lie on his stomach; but "it seemed to puff up with pain like great baby cheeks and he had to roll over on his back to be comfortable" (108). Seemingly in the late stages of pregnancy and fearful of his wife's sexual attraction for her dance instructor, he accuses them of kissing, while "a slow and deadly beat" began "against his stomach walls, as though fists inside him were pleading for attention" (109). When Stern goes to a private rest home, his ulcer has become "a thin, crawling brocade of tenderness that seemed to lay wet on the front of his body." After five weeks there Stern, like any woman in her ninth month of confinement, lugubriously wonders if his stomach will continue to swell until "the flower billowed out too far and burst and everything important ran out of him and there was no more" (134). In another week the ulcer subsides, and Stern goes home.

When Dr. Paul Kay explained these undercurrents in *Stern* to him, Friedman evinced not only surprise but also interest, particularly in the psychosexual substrata of Judaism which the story seems to formulate symbolically. While a perceptive and reflective man, who knows a great deal about himself and others, he was unfamiliar with the unconscious meaning which an ulcer has. A third generation American Jew, he had no inkling of the psychological tensions generated by Judaism, nor of its connection with puberty rites and the bisexuality of human development. He was receptive, however, to the possibility of such residual meanings in what he had written. He has since read widely, if not systematically, in psychology; and his increased awareness of formal explanations of human behavior is evident in the machinery of the play *Scuba Duba*.

These underpinnings of the story have most significance for us in what they define about Friedman's view of man in mid-century America. We would be foolish to claim that Stern in any realistic sense is a typical American. Yet, paradigmatically, in his ambivalent Jewishness, underscored by his bisexuality, he epitomizes the Black Humor protagonist of the 1960's, whose effort to become a part of society is continually thwarted. In the climactic action of the novel, as a gesture toward what he considers to be the practice of the community, Stern challenges the "kike man" to a backyard fight. The sexual overtones which have reverberated in most of Stern's reactions to the "kike man" recur, this time overtly *vis-à-vis*. Stern's feminine role in the encounter restates categorically the indecisiveness of his—and the Black Humor conformist's—accommodation with suburban America.[9]

IV   *Stern's Fantasy World of Violence*

Stern is vulnerable. He wants to think American, to be aggressive, and to be admired by all for his stamina, courage, athletic prowess, and authoritative judgment. But, since he is never quite able to match his thoughts and actions to this ideal, his uncertain status leaves him shadow-boxing fictitious enemies while real toads occupy his imaginary garden. The "kike man" does live down the road; he did shove Stern's wife, whether accidentally or intentionally is never made clear. The mental apprehension of Stern has its real counterpart in the everyday world. Stern walks each moment of his life in a shower of panic,

the corrosive acid of fear dogging his footsteps. His is the cen-
turies-old terror of the Jew, a minority figure, who lived among
pogrom-prone peoples. More representatively, his is this century's
terror of the law-abiding citizen who lives without visible capacity to control his future among the irrational forces of nuclear
world powers, economic booms and busts, and racial militants.

No character in modern fiction leads a mental existence more
violent than Stern. At every turn of his humdrum round of affairs,
he moves like one besieged by superior forces, wary of sudden
attacks and skillful murderous incursions into the citadel of his
puny defenses. Clenched fists, military chants, body-bursting
blows—every kind of mayhem perfected in this century of violence runs riot through Stern's impressionable imagination. No
one walks, enters, or exits in Stern's world; he plunges, flies,
erupts, bursts—movements that imitate the explosive, disruptive
forces of violence. Not since the nineteenth century and the hey-
day of the Darwinian fever has man been conceived of as so
tremblingly naked before the murderous onslaughts of a hostile
environment. Stern must be the most frightened figure in American fiction, for his panic is more profound than the stagy terrors of Charles Brockden Brown's and Edgar Allan Poe's heroes
because it is ultimately more commonplace and everyday.
Perched on the front steps of his house in the evening, his son
on his lap and his great soft body pressed against his wife's hips
for security, Stern feels jittery and isolated—a disturbing, ill-
defined menace surrounding him. Lost is the paradisal pleasure
that was once rural America's of sitting peacefully on the door
stoop to watch the day darken. In the foreword to his anthology
of Black Humor, Friedman comments on the extremes of today's
life. The effect of the bizarre-as-norm on the man in the street is
polarizing: he becomes a frantic Stern or his antidotal contrary,
a representative of "the surprise-proof generation." [10] *Stern* is
Friedman's embodiment of this askew world from the harassed
point of view of one of its reluctant draftees.

Tactics of march and countermarch have filled Stern's mind
since boyhood. As a child, he had lived in terror of an orphan
boy who he imagined would someday "appear suddenly in an
alley with a great laugh, fling Stern against a wall, lift him high,
and drop him down, steal his jacket in the cold, and run away
with it, come back, and punch Stern's eyes to slits" (51). His

grandmother was jokingly supposed to have "a whole mob" of other old ladies "organized" (60). His uncles would sing the prayers at Passover as if they were "militant chants." His Uncle Mackie, with "bronzed, military-trim body" would do "a series of heroic-sounding but clashing chants" with "great clangor" as if to "enlist a faction to his banner and start a split Seder" (57–58).

As an adult, Stern cowers in abject fear at imaginary reprisals of the "kike man." He avoids driving past the "kike man's" house, "afraid that the man would pull him out of the car and break his stomach" (49). In retaliation, Stern dreams of crushing the "kike man" with a blow "battering his head through his living-room window" (102), or of catching the "kike man's" little boy on the bumpers of his car and then of driving the mile to his own house in seconds and of disappearing undetected into his garage. But the thought of the "kike man's" counterattack paralyzes him: "He pictured a car fight in which the man would get Stern's boy, following him onto the lawn and pinning him against the drain-pipe, while Stern, waiting upstairs, held his hands over his ears, blocking out the noise. The man would then, somehow, pick off Stern's wife in her kitchen and then drive upstairs and finish off Stern himself, cringing in his bedroom" (50).

The "kike man" is named De Luccio. Checking in the telephone book, Stern discovers that there are eighteen other De Luccios in town. Immediately he concedes to himself that even "if he were to defeat the man, an army of relatives stood by to take his place" (50). The sight of the man "wearing a veteran's jacket" makes Stern's throat turn over: "It meant he had come through the worst part of the Nomandy campaign, knew how to hold his breath in foxholes for hours at a time and then sneak out to slit a throat in silence. He was skilled as a foot fighter and went always with deadly accuracy to a man's groin" (52–53). And Stern saw the man "a light sleeper, nerves sharpened by combat, waiting, coiled and ready to leap forward and slit throats with commando neatness" (54). In desperation Stern wonders if his being blind, flanked by his wife and child, would protect him from the man's assault, a bone-jarring "judo chop" and a sickening kick in the crotch (93–94).

Apart from the contretemps with the "kike man," the normal round of Stern's life is an endless fantasy of cringing self-defense.

His assistant at the office, an effeminate young man, always appears to Stern to be darting menacingly, body coiled "with vicious ballet grace," toward his desk. Fearful of being reported to a Board of Good Taste for having an ulcer—a "dirty, Jewish, unsophisticated" malady—Stern longs instead for "dueling scars and broken legs suffered while skiing" (88). He hesitates to admonish a baby-sitter for teaching his son about God, "afraid she would come after him one night with a torch-bearing army of gentiles and tie him to a church" (112). The innocent assurance of the doctor who examines his ulcer that "we don't have to go in there" conjures up for Stern a vision "of entire armadas of men and equipment trooping into his stomach and staying there a long time" (80). And the stabs of pain in his ulcerated duodenum become fists steadily stepping up the rhythm of their beat within him (110).

The same fantasy of punitive constraint pursues Stern like a Fury when he goes to the Grove Rest Home. The somber New England air of the place makes Stern, the good citizen, self-conscious of his Semitic genesis and certain that the founders would veto him "with clenched fists" (115) in spite of his desire to be a loyal American. Informed that milk and cookies are served at five, with only one tardiness allowed, Stern reflects that "even were he to flee to the Netherlands after a milk and cookie infraction, getting a fifteen-hour start," the crippled Negro attendant, with "great jaw muscles," "would go after him Porgy-like and catch him eventually" (117).

The patients terrify him, particularly a tall "erupting," "grenade-like youth" whom Stern jumpily keeps expecting to smash him in sudden "swiftly changing mood" (138–39). When two baseball teams come to the rest home to play a benefit game, Stern excitedly substitutes for an outfielder who has been hit with a line drive; but at bat, facing the pitcher, he is fearful that a bean ball is "planned to put a bloodflower between his eyes" (141). Sneaking out one night with two other patients for some beers and a tryst with a girl, Stern trembles, certain that the instant they passed the gate the Negro orderly would have them "picked up in trucks and initiate punitive measures" (145). The girl looks like "a battered Puerto Rican caricature of Gene Tierney" "after a session with two longshoremen who'd been paid to rough her up a little, not to kill her but to change her face around a little" (136, 145).

There is no escape for Stern, no place to hide. Neither convalescence nor work or home life offers him a haven. He crouches in his office, locks himself in the toilet stall—hiding in uncontrollable panic from the confident steps of his boss in the morning. The phone ring slices at him like a knife. His house awaits him, "an enemy that sucked oil and money and posted a kike-hating sentry down the street" (174). Even in the refuge of his bed, his thoughts are invaded by "numb and choking fear" (173).

Stern lives in a "stifled, desperate" (171) world that knows no primal cause and effect, a world ruled over by a Mosaic dispensation run amok, the Judaic law of an eye for an eye swollen to horrifying, bizarre proportions. Stern dreams of his Negro friend Battleby flinging off his horn-rim glasses and filling "an open-cab truck with twenty bat-carrying Negro middle-weights, bare to the waist and glistening with perfect musculature," to do battle with the "kike man" (96). The usual scale of values is tipped into frightening ratios. Man trembles before the accusing eye of a traffic cop, but he indulges complacently the excesses and enormities of the Mafia. All the time that he is decrying mass racial extermination, individual cruelty is losing significance.

Stern reacts to the real and imagined dangers of every day with a mental life of sexual aggression and finally, in the climactic stages of his nervous breakdown, with violent actions. He is the little man on the street, one of the vox populi of this century, through whose eyes and ears has been refracted too much violence and pretense. Hollywood and Madison Avenue's exploitation of love as a commodity to be huckstered has left Stern obsessed with sexual nightmares of his wife's infidelity. He runs "with teeth clenched through a crowded train station, as though he were a quarterback going downfield, lashing out at people with his elbows, bulling along with his shoulders." To outraged complaints, he hollers, "I didn't see you. You're insignificant-looking" (179). He sasses a traffic cop, lecturing him when stopped for a traffic violation, "Is this your idea of a crime? With what's going on in this country—rape and everything?" He accosts unapproachable women.

In *Stern,* Friedman portrays the end product of this century's assault on the human sensibility. Man's private and public lives run on separate treadmills these days. A bland noncommittal exterior masks a ferocious fantasy life. Outward acquiescence in a dehumanized society reduces the inner life to catatonic silence or to jangling disconnected protest. Stern's affliction is mainly the latter.

V *The Language of* Stern

Friedman's nervous prose is highly suggestive of violence. The frequency of active verbs has the fictional characters twitching as energetically and erratically as high-speed, machine-driven marionettes. Henry James's people *swim* into rooms; Friedman's, as we have already noted, *fly* through them to signify that violence is the keystone of our ideology, the trademark of our frontier heritage, the drama of our Western mythology, and the epistemology of our Declaration of Independence. Guns are sold, no questions asked, through mail-order houses. Fathers train their sons in good citizenship by giving them a rifle when they come of age. This matter-of-fact acceptance of violence as a cultural ideal is less satirized than parodied in stunned disbelief by Friedman, and a pervasive metaphor in the narrative is that of war. Stern's mind and body are portrayed as a no-man's-land populated with the sophisticated hardware of modern combat. He reels continually from actual and imagined blows of civilization. Like Tennyson's "Nature, red in tooth and claw," [11] his ulcer attacks him "coarse-tufted, sharp-toothed" (82). Entire armadas of men and equipment troop into his stomach and bivouac there.

Significantly, Stern's fantasies of fright often revert atavistically to the bare fists of savage reprisal. The friendly handshake has metamorphosed in his daily nightmare into an ubiquitous fist that threatens his existence in crescendoing multiples. When Stern refrains from contradicting a Negro taxi driver, he is fearful of being backed "against a fender, and cut . . . to ribbons with lethal combinations" (83) of fisticraft. The gentlemanly rules of pugilistic defense do not apply in Stern's imagined world, for the gangland law and fights of big-city ghettos prevail. Stern's father carries a jagged scar on the ridge of his nose, one given to him one day "by two soccer players in a strange neighborhood who had suddenly lashed out and knocked him unconscious" (85). A recurrent hallucination of Stern's depicts him as the victim of ordinary people—drugstore countermen, for example, who suddenly mobilize according to an attack plan and trap Stern in a store against the paperback books, insanely "hitting him in the stomach a few times and then holding him for a paid-off patrolman" (85).

The symbolic action of such hallucinations is obvious. Friedman conceives of man ironically as having regressed to a lawless state in response to an overstructured civilization. The monolithic impersonality of a technocracy communicates to man no sense of his belonging to a group. He has become an outsider, groping in terror for signs that will relate him to his world. Out of a desperate will to survive, he slips into a new savagery—a vivid but cruel Alice-in-Wonderland where sadistic Red Queens and Mad Hatters force him, like Alice, to reformulate continually his assumptions about people and manners. The actual has been abandoned for a mental world that more accurately reflects reality; illogic and mystery have succeeded reason and clarity. "Were you ever a magician before you became my father?" the sexually incompetent Stern is asked by his son. "Right before" (186), Stern answers with the starkness of things seen through the looking glass.

Charles Dickens, an early diagnostician of the ills of the industrial milieu, saw with bitter dread the distinction between human and nonhuman blurring: the factory system was rendering man in the image of its mass-produced products; machines were acquiring minds. Dickens' perception of things to come has arrived for Friedman, for our tacit aquiescence in the sameness of men and machinery is envisioned by Friedman as a profound human ingestion of things, with the stomach and the brain most vulnerable to this modern disease of transubstantiation. Under the nervous tension of living near the "kike man," Stern's stomach proteanlike alters into one piece of cloth after another: hot brocade, tablecloth, parachute. During his nervous breakdown his head becomes "a leaky basement which Stern patrolled from the inside, running over with plaster each time a picture of the man down the street threatened to slide in through a crack. One night, the basement leaked in so many places he could not get to them all" (185). At other times "a motor, powered by rocket fuels, ran at a dementedly high idle somewhere between his shoulder blades" (172). The crippled Negro orderly at the Grove Rest Home moves clatteringly forward; his "leg sections rasping and grinding" (116), he is a demonic "man with a machine shop going full blast below his waist" (142)—or so he appears to the indoctrinated perception of Stern. Man's traditional means of retreat from the horrors of profane existence by escape into an inner life of the spirit is rehearsed in the pathetic gesture of Stern's fantasies; but now man finds his mind, once a sanctuary, a terrifying electronics reflector of the flotsam and jetsam of a technological age that is interminably at war. The Red Queen has altered to the "kike man'" and the Mad Hatter to the Negro orderly; but the psychotic delirium of Stern's world, like the logical illogicality of Alice's, continues to be the real world.

VI *Friedman's Achievement*

Stern is a first novel of great promise. Like J. D. Salinger, who miraculously melded the unpromising materials of some short stories into *The Catcher in the Rye,* Friedman has united some *New Yorker* sketches into a novel disturbing in its power to move us.

In *Stern,* Friedman accepts the risk that the mundane and the unattractive always pose for art. Like the "Pop artist," he dares to gaze on the puerilities of our supermarket culture with the avid eyes of a bargain-basement shopper. No gimcrack is so tasteless or so limited that his esthetic eye cannot envision its representative function in a world inhabited by his thoroughly urbanized imagination. He is bent on describing the frightened efforts of Everyman to relate to this dime-store environment; but, by its very nature, the five-and-ten-cent store resists definition. A "blank confusion . . . of trivial objects," Wordsworth named the London of his day,[12] despairing of the mind's capacity to encompass it imaginatively; and the labyrinthine New York City of Stern is equally intractable to the frightened, disorderly minds of this century.

Mid-twentieth-century America has grown so paradoxically disparate in its inane sameness that it would now defy the assimilative powers of Theodore Dreiser. The social Realism of the 1930's of James Farrell and John Dos Passos was the last successful effort at comprehensiveness of detail. Today, such an attempt leads to the gargantuan ruin that is found in William Gaddis' *The Recognitions*. Yet, Friedman perseveres in this social Realist tradition, with the difference that he is not afraid to use the terse style of the caricaturist. Unlike the omnibus methods of Barth, Pynchon, and Nabokov, who assimilate knowledge wholesale, Friedman dares to conceive of his diverse materials in a few basic shapes. On this economical structure he superimposes, as if so many found objects, the manners of the New York middle class that he knows best.

Because of this special ambience, we can easily overlook the wider applicability of Friedman's vision. Friedman is defining the *Massenmensch*, mass man, of the twentieth century who shares with his fellow beings no tradition, no feelings and habits of thought, no great rhythms of life and death; he enjoys none of what Alfred Kazin in writing of Sholom Aleichem's people has called "the unconscious wealth of humanity, which is its memory," "that deep part of your life [which] is lived below the usual level of strain, of the struggle for values, of the pressing and harrowing need . . . to define your values all over again in each situation." [13] Stern does not relish his identity as do Sholom Aleichem's *shtetl* Jews or Dickens' London Cockneys. His *Angst* epitomizes the despair of a consumer society that renders its past obsolete with every tin can it discards.

For all its conventional social furniture and comic manner, Friedman's vision of mass man in *Stern* carries the conviction of deeply felt experience. He accepts the unlovable features of Stern and dares to limn them with all the authentic details of close observation that is one of his fictional strengths. His journalistic training supports him well in his depiction of the selfish, chimera-cluttered existence of ordinary man.

Friedman's surface of disordered triviality is deceptively laconic. It masks deep reservations of feeling, of muted hostility, of sublimated desires. To realize such extensions of meaning, he has mastered a highly suggestive idiom. Stern's illness becomes symptomatic of a whole culture—of a daily round so dissociated that a nursing home for cripples serves as its objective correlative. Only among other mutilated victims of modernity, among the dismembered and the trepanned, Friedman asseverates indecorously, does contemporary man like Stern, who suffers neurotically from a flatulent, empty existence, find human fellowship.

CHAPTER 3

A Mother's Kisses

WHETHER RIGHTLY or wrongly, the first half of the twentieth century geared its understanding of the psyche to the teachings of Freud. Oedipus complex, id, ego, superego, the "exhaustion of weaning" (to quote from W. H. Auden's "Petition"), all the attendant empirical postulates provided the age with categorical constructs as central to its patterns of thought as those of time and space. Sex was documented as a furtive object of leers and backseat gropings, a prurient product of the puritanical climate of America, packaged in Hollywood and merchandized on Madison Avenue. With a body of Venus and with a little-girl face and voice of adolescence, love was elevated to an ideal that continually titillated but never satisfied. Inevitably, sex acquired in the underground life of America a salacious importance, divorced from the natural rhythms of generation, birth and death, and from the family relationships of father, mother, and child.

In *Stern*, Friedman explores the tremors of civil terror, while snickering *en passant* at the rubric of the insatiable American wife and her inadequate husband. In his second novel *A Mother's Kisses*, published two years later, in 1964, Friedman is concerned directly with this and a good many other sexual fixations, as he scrutinizes our preoccupation with what Philip Wylie several decades ago denounced as "Momism." In a lampoon of our mythology of sex, Friedman tabulates our fascination with incest taboos, sex goddesses, vacation romances, French girls, panty raids, adolescent libidos, aging sirens, and superannuated satyrs. Yet the solvent of laughter does not entirely conceal that he seems disconcertingly at the same time to take seriously the case for our sexual traumas.

I *Joseph*

Joseph, a seventeen-year-old Stern, and his raucous mother Meg act out a one-reel flicker in *A Mother's Kisses* as a sequel to the daguerrotypes taken of them in *Stern*. There's is a Mack Sennett comedy of the trials of coming of age in the Jewish lower-middle-class enclave of Bensonhurst, Brooklyn. Stern suffers recurrent anguish because he has not mastered the manners of suburbia; Joseph also worries about being in step with his peer group. His is the anxiety of the conventional soul who wishes to be part of the gang but uneasily suspects that it is laughing at him. He is a teen-age Prufrock—gauche in dating etiquette, limited in dance technique, and fearful of neighborhood toughs.

Joseph is the only one of his friends not yet accepted into college for the fall term. His immediate concern, then, is to wangle admittance somewhere despite crowded classrooms and expanding enrollments and, once that is accomplished, to cope with the mysteries of room-hunting, girl-chasing, and course-dodging. Complicating this teen-age crisis for Joseph is the fact that he is divided in his desire to go away to college. As if to ensure his not having to leave home, he applies to only two schools: Bates and Columbia. Bates quickly turns down his application, which leaves all his hopes pinned on Columbia. No other out-of-town college inexplicably appeals to him; he just cannot bring himself to apply to the many places across the country that he can think of—Duke, Bowdoin, Colgate, Bucknell, Brown, Cornell, Carnegie Tech, and Oberlin—to name a few he considers and dismisses.

Unhappy but helpless, he looks to the inspired assistance of his mother Meg to decide for him. She is equally reluctant, however, to see him leave the maternal nest; instead, to distract him, she engineers his employment at a summer resort. The ruse back-fires when he is assigned to the camp waiters ("a bunch of four-teen-year-old bed-wetters" [34]),[1] who merely work for their room and board, instead of to the professional waiters, who actually earn money. After a few weeks, Joseph is sent home in disgrace, having been caught rummaging through the suitcases of the other waiters. Having learned that Columbia had rejected his application, he had felt the desperate need to create a tragic situation to demonstrate his plight. Eventually, Meg accepts the inevitable; and through the influence of one of her multitudinous acquaintances, she wedges him into Kansas Land Grant Agricultural. She insists on accompanying him to that far-off place, ostensibly to help him find lodging. Instead, she wangles a room for them in a crowded hotel in the college boom town by playing on the lurid imagination of the desk clerk; she claims that she and Joseph "were lovers and just had this one night together" before she had to get back to her "old man so he shouldn't suspect anything" (207). And there they live week after week while Joseph tries diffidently to get her to go home and while she schemes to get him to return with her. When he was five, Joseph was watched during the summer by a Negro woman who kept him tethered to a twenty-foot chain. The habit of wheeling at the end of an imaginary umbilical cord has also been the story of Joseph's first seventeen years.

Besides the usual adolescent *Angst* about social standing and a college future, Joseph has been agitated by sexual longings imprecisely aimed at his nubile older sister and his hippy, big-breasted mother—the two females with whom he has been unavoidably in daily intimate contact during his formative teen-age years. In Joseph's jejune sexual yearnings, Friedman enunciates some dark human urges that man has fearfully hedged with taboos. Libidinous feelings as he glimpses his sister undressing in the tight quarters of their three-room apartment disturb Joseph with guilty thoughts that he is committing infractions against the rules, against powerful if ill-defined strictures. Decorum permits a boy to have physical contact with an older sister, even in the excitement of an occasion to find his arm wedged in her cleavage; but, Joseph wonders, with sudden stiffening, "whether he was supposed to enjoy it" (63).

Joseph inhabits a female world of mother, sister, aging aunt, and cleaning woman. His earliest sexual awakenings are associated with his sister, and his memory of their growing up together was of their seeming "to circle one another in a great dampness." For years as a boy he had lain awake in the dinette where his bed was made up at night, waiting for her to return from a date and possibly undress within his view. She ordinarily used the bathroom; but "on occasion she would reward his vigil by flinging off her clothes in the foyer" of the living room, where she slept. He remembered with excitement one early morning when she had decided "to examine her breasts by lamplight, serving up first one and then the other, studying them quizzically as though they were twin world atlases." To Joseph, her breasts were New Worlds of feminine mystery which, Columbus-like, he greedily discovered across the stellar longitude of the living room.

Less arcane was his introduction another night to the bodily impurities of female flesh, when "she stood nude for a minute and worked on a behind pimple." He was not sure if he liked that session although, "if pressed, he guessed he would have to admit he was glad it had come off." His initiation into the erotic intimacy of being alone in an apartment at night with a woman happened to him with his sister. She sat in an armchair. "coiled and moist in her slip," polishing her toenails, and telling him a dirty joke, "while he walked in and out of the room, trying to catch his breath."

It is no wonder that his earliest erotic dreams concentrate on his sister: "He had a recurring dream in which she settled comfortably in his bed and allowed him to explore her body, her face sweet, patient, neutral. He loved the dream, wishing he could arrange to have it run on schedule. Sometimes, late at night, in lieu of an undressing, she would come and stand alongside his bed, eating some cookies, stooping to touch his hair. He had a hanging, half-awake shred of a memory involving cold, wet, milky, low and lassoing half-mad kisses in the darkness" (143). The physical proximity of brother and sister during the time of dawning sexual interest lends an inevitable prurience to their relationship. It is not difficult to understand why society has hedged equally strong taboos around such relationships, until the primordial feeling about incest communicates an unhealthy emotion about all sex. These truths, which are so distasteful that we forbid them the conscious level of our thoughts, Friedman has dared to drag out of their psychic hiding places where society has desperately willed their incarceration. He merrily reminds us that our chilling adult sexual obsessions were once our happy childhood fantasies. With insouciant irreverence, he will not let us forget that the inhibition of sexual curiosity is a product of societal and of familial taboos.

Joseph acts out the phantoms of our haunted imaginations. Behind the locked door of the bathroom, he inhales the flannel of a pair of his sister's pajamas; then he slips into them for a minute of breathtaking transvestism. He lies on the floor, pretending a childhood game, to peek up the dress of the Negro cleaning woman, moved by the erotic mystery of miscegenation. He reacts with fear to the sexual undercurrent that fertilizes anti-Semitic hatred. He responds lewdly to his mother's voluptuous girl friend when she appears clad "warm and breakfasty in her bathrobe," barely camouflaging a body innocent of bra and with panties "a fleck of redness" which he cannot be sure are panties at all. Joseph is justifiably bewildered about the protocol of handling her indiscrete leg-revealings, for manners condone her improprieties while social taboos limit his reactions to her provocative gestures. So Joseph prays "for another bathrobe separation" and wonders "what would happen if he suddenly swooped in through the opening and got at her legs for a few seconds. Would it be glossed over with a few admonitions or would he actually be dragged into court to face charges?" (96–98).

II *Joseph and Meg*

Most bewildering for Joseph are the emotions he feels for his mother. Meg is a henna-rinsed, pneumatic female, stoutly corseted and mascaraed, loud of voice, uninhibited of thought, and blatant in word and deed. She inhabits a make-believe theatrical world of the 1920's that is bounded by the patter of tin-pan alley and by the intricate dance steps of the Aragon Ballroom. Joseph remembers a time in his boyhood when she "had done a great deal of voluptuous midday lying around," "Massive-breasted in a white brassiere," with Joseph bringing her drinks of soda. "She doesn't act like a mother" (139), one of his friends had remarked, coming upon her lounging on her back in the living room.

Joseph's relationship with his mother is a combination of reluctant gigolo and dependent son. She gives him ear kisses that are reminiscent of those the sexy French girl at summer camp gave him on the dance floor; at other times her kisses, "wide, and gurgling," feel "as though a large, freshly exposed, open-meloned internal organ had washed against his face" (181). Joseph recoils from them much as Huck Finn does from similar moves of fondness on Aunt Polly's part. Meg's buying Joseph a suit becomes a Third Avenue Yiddish farce about an unfaithful housewife putting clothes on the back of her lover with nickels and

dimes scrimped from her grocery money. In Joseph's eyes, his
mother's flamboyant sexuality marks her as a target for every
two-bit sex artist they encounter; and his reaction pushes him
into the role of the outraged consort who defends his lady's honor.

The final section of the novel, which describes Joseph's efforts
to orient himself to the strange, motherless world of college,
brings his dependency on her to a temporary, if not conclusive,
termination. At first, Meg accompanies him everywhere, even to
a fraternity rush dinner; and she appears at Joseph's first class,
bringing him a sweater to wear. She accompanies Joseph to the
movies, where all around them young couples are necking.
"Would you hold your mother's hand," she asks. "I would," he
answers, "but what's the point?" (230). More and more, however,
he slips out alone.

But Meg does not surrender without a fight. Late one night,
when he returns from an unsuccessful evening of girl-chasing,
she greets him in their hotel room with fresh lipstick on, in high
heels and slip, a Scotch highball in hand, with the faint aura in
the room of a lover just departed. "Come over her and give me
a love and I'll soothe you," she says provocatively. "Come," she
said, taking his head, "I just made a lap. You know your mother
could always provide you with a fast good time where no one
else could. He's worried about girls. I showed a woman in the
bar your picture and she was amazed I could just sit there
calmly, like a normal person, not making a fuss, with a son that
looks like that. Come over here fast and I'll be your social life"
(268–69).

Joseph tries half-heartedly to free himself from her suffocating
embrace. He rakes up all his childhood grudges against her, reminding her of the "long, gray afternoons she had forced him to
spend in corsetieres' anterooms while she climbed in and out of
Merry Widows," and of "the champagne dance contests she had
forced him to enter each summer as her lindy-hop partner at
Hirsch's Seaside Cottages" (270–71). It frustrates him, however,
that "the stories seemed more nostalgic than enraged." Meg's
reaction is that of the eternal female bemused by the futile
flutterings of her impaled lover. "I let you recite, you had fun,
now come over here fast," she says, "because if I don't get a kiss
I'll tear your face off from your cuteness. Who knew about such

a mouth? Get down here with your lips or there'll be all-out war" (270).

When the spectre of her infidelities is alluded to, she drops the role of coquette and becomes the offended mother, bent on departing for home in the morning. Guilty tingles curl through Joseph, and he assures his mother that he did not mean she had to go that soon. The next morning, in striking contrast to the erotic image she had projected the night before, she looms maternally above him, "stale and bedraggled in a bathrobe, eyes still sealed with sleep, a cigarette bouncing on her bottom lip," holding an armload of freshly ironed clothing for him (273). The upshot of their quarrel is that she continues on from week to week, but she suddenly one day accepts the separation as inevitable. On the morning of her departure, Joseph notices admiringly how robust his mother looks. "Stay another few days" (285), he says, as he cuts French class to take her to the train.

It is small wonder that Joseph is confused by the ambivalence of his feelings for his mother. If he kisses her when he is not feeling well and for comfort puts his head on her shoulder, he finds himself shamelessly smelling her sweater. Her gratifying embrace dredges up from the depths of him "a mysterious cry" (85) that unsettles him again. When he bends over her bed to kiss her neck as he leaves for his first day of classes at college, he feels "great blasts of heat stealing up from beneath the covers," reminding him of the times that he would get "into bed with her years back on Sunday mornings, finding it black and stovelike and never being sure he wanted to be under there with her" (223). Growing up with the perennial dishabille of Meg and her girl friends has convinced Joseph that he has never seen "middle-aged women unless they were in foundation garments" (33).

Sex for Joseph has been, therefore, a furtive thing of joyless voyeurism, of matronly females with menstrual cramps and giant thighs, wet kisses and alarming breast nipples. Still, his dependence on the bosomy presence of his mother is so great that he toys for one desperate moment with the idea of her staying with him at college for one semester. But his resentment at this dependence is often murderous in intent. As she stands near the hotel room window in her nightgown, he has a sudden desire to push her out, a compulsion so intense he begins to perspire.

Graphically, he fancies her flipping end over end or dropping "pancake style, to the pavement." When he least expected it, the thought would come to mind; and "He would wonder how long it would take her to fall, was there a chance someone would catch her, was it mandatory that her face be smashed up or might it go relatively unmangled" (232).

Thus, Meg's motherly kisses are both a source of comfort to Joseph and a cause of his disquiet. As a stereotype of the doting Jewish mother, they are an object of Friedman's laughter; and, as a sign of her and Joseph's emotional crisis, they are a synopsis of his psychosexual insights. A measure of Friedman's perception is that he is not blind to the vital sources of our person that are residual in the clichés of our existence; and another measure of his artistry is that he forces us, like the Pop artist, to look at these objects as if for the first time—to see their thingness as it was before an overlay of routine meanings dulled our senses to them.

In the larger structural units of the novel, Friedman is equally adept at marshaling his narrative materials into a statement of the Oedipal theme. The postwar difficulty of getting into college becomes equivalent to the male child's struggle to gain his freedom from maternal domination. At the same time, however, Friedman is careful to keep the story uppermost. Since indirection is a virtue he consciously seeks, the symbolic action of the narrative never becomes obtrusive, never usurps the primary attention, as it does in Bernard Malamud's myth-laden *The Natural*.

III   *The Malaise of Feeling*

Friedman treats specifically of overprotective mother love, but he takes all modern aberrations of feelings as his fictional provenance. He defines for us the unspoken horror of family antagonisms and the pretzel-like entanglements of human friendships. He isolates the empty enthralment of film romance and the orgiastic monotony of adolescent emotion. He labels the predatory sexual instinct of love for its object and the obscene hope of the parent for his child. Although love is inherently tragic in its consequences, Friedman permits no such noble passion to distill his laughter at its antic disposition. For him, Venus is inexorably a sexually unsatisfied wife; Cupid, a dirty-mouthed urchin; Diana, a puzzled adolescent. Shorn of its platonic and romantic trappings, love reduces to a physical appetite that is bewildering in its emotional confusion of sexual desire with maternal security and that is frightening in its voracious meld with the other psychic hungers of cruelty, hatred, envy, and dread.

From the seasonal cycles re-enacted by pre-Hellenic vegetation cults to the annual summer Coca-Cola advertisements, man has celebrated sex as a communal obligation; he has conceived of it as an ontological principle with love as its mystique; and he has overlaid it with ritual, sanctifying its expenditure of energy with words and sentiments until the machinery of the act is either identified with its end product or, contrariwise, eliminated in an alembic of idealization. Modern man has so blinded himself with the gadgetry of a world of make-believe emotions that he tends to be forgetful of the peculiar defenselessness of love. Such self-hypnosis arouses Friedman to laughter, and he insists that we join him. He reminds us that to feel, to participate in love, is to be vulnerable. The sharpness of his laughter forces us to recognize our common human plight.

Friedman's pathetic girl-women speak in a pastiche of *femme-fatale* roles. The Puerto Rican girl in *Stern* talks with inflated sentiments like an ingenue who has not quite mastered her part and lapses with disconcerting frequency into her natural argot. "Now, my knighted author," she trills to Stern, "will you be with me on the highest of all levels?" With contraceptive in hand, she steers him to the bed. "Then thrill my secret fibers," she pleads; but she also warns him in the familiar terms of the prostitute, "Now, honey, don't spoil it. Really, let's do a good one" (153–54). The teen-age French girl with whom Joseph dances at the summer camp chatters frenziedly into his ear in the presumed patois of the toughly tender, sophisticated siren of a Grade-B Humphrey Bogart film:

"I'm a French girl, but when I got here they had a nurse named Frenchie so they made up the name Portugee. I went to a party just before I left, where a famous celebrity got me in a corner and stripped me down with his eyes. Once I had an operation and woke up to find my breasts numbered 'one' and 'two' over my hospital nightgown. Things are always happening to me. The floor waxer at home once asked me if I could lift my skirt a little while he sat on the couch and did a little something with himself. He said he'd gotten that way by hanging around with racetrack women." (31)

But Friedman never lets us forget that beneath the paper-thin poise breathes a callow, uncertain teen-ager trying to grow up too fast. The adolescent world of A Mother's Kisses differs from that of J. D. Salinger's Catcher in the Rye in this respect. Childhood innocence holds no ideal significance for Friedman because it does not exist for him. Reality, as he sees it, is the profound gesture of every man to be like his neighbor. His adolescents do not reject the phony world of adults in a desperate ploy to retain their honesty and simplicity; instead, they ape their elders with a fumbling avidity that reveals in its embarrassing affirmation the obscenity and violence that form the core of our amenities. In laying bare to our gaze the state of things, Friedman reveals a complex intention at work in fiction that is topical in its Pop language and yet recondite in its social Realism.

The erotic appeals to youth today, creating in them intolerable tensions which we then deplore, is a basic theme of A Mother's Kisses. Despite the humor of the situation, we recognize and sympathize with Joseph's naive self-deprecation when he is led by a French girl to believe that he has aroused in her "the feeling only swarthy fellows named Hernando" should be able to stimulate. Disbelieving his powers of erotic suggestion, he wonders "if in some accidental way he had not brushed against her European hotbone, whatever that was" (32). Joseph accepts the cliché "European lover" as a norm toward which, he like all American males, must stumble, even as he contrariwise accepts without question the notion that he is a fumbling, inadequate sexual partner. The chasm between adult and adolescent worlds is wide; yet youth frenziedly tries to throw a bridge across it to get at the imagined treasures in the wondrous land of their parents. Meg's flamboyant sexuality, her salacious innuendos in front of Joseph, her physically provocative Irish girl friend—all entice Joseph into frantic conjectures about the sketchily known female. Hence, when he has the chance to explore the body of a compliant Viennese mental case, he breathlessly approaches her "as though she were a wonderful store": "He made a furtive examination of her body, not so much enjoying the touches as collecting them like baseball cards, each breast a Bill Dickey, her behind a pair of Stan Musials. He asked her choked questions as he roamed her body, adding her answers to his pile" (54).

The serpent in this paradise, however, is that society's ideals and its prohibitions often contradict each other. Thus, Joseph feels like a thief in taking advantage of the girl. At the same time that he is telling himself that "her body was too good to waste," he reveals his fears of social disapproval with the thought that she was probably going back into a mental institution "and that would seal her lips forever, in case she ever decided to get back at him and spill everything to his folks." She represents to him a wonderful store; but he is bent on theft and feels pressed as though "he had four minutes to take anything he wanted before the owner came back from dinner." Fear of penalties for infractions of the rules constantly inhibits Joseph; and since he never finishes his sexual gambits, disappointment is his usual award. For all the chances he takes with the Viennese girl, he learns to his dismay only the dismal truth about the close anatomical link between oral and anal orifices. Whenever he touches an erogenous zone of the girl, she cranes her head back, letting loose with a cry that sounds like "a sudden plumbing defect in a far-off house at midnight" (46). Thus is Joseph instructed that love and the mystery of creation are somehow allied to the excrescence of death and the modern mechanics of disposal which lead a life of their own.

Friedman is documenting the contemporary worship of sex—all its bizarre manifestations—with the zeal of a sociologist and with the irreverence of the stand-up comic. The accepted practice of necking in a darkened movie house metamorphoses under his scrutiny into a titanic thrashing about of a whaling captain, "holding the tiller of a longboat and weaving back and forth in a stormy sea," while a groaning girl—the stricken whale presumably —tries "to keep a strand of blond hair in place at the same time" that she receives her date's "deep, plunging kisses" (230). To remain immaculately coiffured, so all the advertisements aver, is to retain purity and respect regardless of a sweaty, precarious, supine position. Friedman sees the inherent flaw in such reasoning as an inevitable product of the weird never-never land of topsy-turvy values of mid-twentieth-century American culture.

One of the popular transmitters of this culture is the cinema. Friedman believes that many of his own attitudes were formed by the movies he saw as a boy growing up in the late 1930's and early 1940's. The Hollywood stars and the scenes of their amours of that era furnish him with part of his fictional vocabulary. In his play *Steambath*, he has one of the characters express such a sentiment: "I suppose it never occurred to you that every smile, every whisper, every puff of a cigarette taken by my generation was inspired by the forties' movie. That my generation wouldn't know how to mix a drink, drive a car, kiss a girl, straighten a tie—if it weren't for Linda Darnell and George Brent . . . That the sole reason for my generation's awkward floundering in the darkness is that Zachary Scott is gone . . . and I assure you that Dennis Hopper is no substitute. . . ."[2]

Friedman sees Joseph—like most adolescents—as nurtured on this scale of values. Much of the time Joseph is trying to mask his jejune feelings by borrowing the context of a sophisticated world for them; but he is still the schoolboy, destined to betray his manners in some awkward movement, as Friedman makes clear in a trope descriptive of him and the French girl dancing: "She began to kiss his ear, to strain against him as they danced, Joseph holding her in an astonished manner, as though she were a pan of water he was carrying to wash the blackboards" (31).

The movies are for Joseph a truer reality than the frustrating everyday world he inhabits. They provide his otherwise disjunctive life with consecutiveness, with tragic and comic significance. His real, if untidy and inchoate, emotions acquire meaning for him only when they are given voice in the melodramatic terms of Hollywood. Joseph often translates the intolerable ache of his adolescent uncertainty into the familiar celluloid world of organized daydreams. Thus, the little strumpet of a French girl at summer camp, who is herself acting out a make-believe role, appears to him like the heroine of a Merry-Widow operetta, "her eyes startled as though invisible Cyril Ritchards were fawning alongside of her whispering delicious courtroom gossip in her ear," and her voice sounded as if it were "coming from a small French music box, in the guest room of a château in Nancy." Joseph imagines her "as having an aging, widowed Louis Jourdan of a dad, nursing him along through a web of affairs with a drawing room wisdom beyond her years" (31).

Even when Joseph has the bad news from Columbia University that his application has been rejected, he says, "Oh Christ," and shakes his head, "feeling he had to make an obvious demonstration of disappointment for an invisible crowd that expected such things. He went back into the cabin and lay on the bed, trying to work up a few tears, helping them along by letting his shoulders tremble, in the style of actresses called upon to convey sorrow with their backs to the camera" (70–71). Joseph wonders "why he could react to tragedy only with movie routines" (71).

As a sociopsychological Realist, Friedman is saying that we are products of our civilization in unexpected ways that stun us with their appositeness. Isolated in our urban centers of multi-lithic stone from participation in the elemental rhythms of nature—of spring, summer, and fall; of seeding, growth, and harvest; of the daily round of tasks geared to the daylight hours—we have substituted new dimensionless cycles of life such as the ninety-minute, full-length feature. And the feelings we have are as arbitrary and as deficient as the fragmentary blurbs on the marquees of our cinema-oriented culture. These equally exaggerated and stunted tags of our affective lives give visible form to the dialectics of the electronic age, which Friedman dramatizes in his fable of Joseph's summer of discontent.

IV *Meg*

The courage that Friedman shows generally in his exploration (to use Mailer's words) "up the upper Amazon of the inner eye" [3] is considerable so long as he limits himself to the haunted viewpoint of Stern or to the umbilically tethered eyes of Joseph. Just as it is for Stern and Joseph, the female psyche seems to be for Friedman a fathomless cave of terrifying dimensions and elusive windings. He does not look closely at Stern's wife; and, although Meg looms large—almost the central figure—in *A Mother's Kisses,* he takes none of the risks with her he does with Stern and Joseph.

Hints are not wanting, however, that a deep-seated sexual malaise disturbs Meg. There are her passive nonentity of a husband; her adulterous indiscretions during the early years of her marriage; and the inexplicable, psychosomatic collapses into invalidism of both her and her husband. For weeks at a time she had flopped around the house in a bathrobe or lain phlegmatically on the living room couch, "Massive-breasted in a white brassière" (139); and once her husband had not moved from a bedboard for over two years. There are her blatant physicality, loud brassiness, hennaed hair, mascaraed eyes, youthful dress, and little-girl gyrations—all conveying in her effort at gregariousness a courageously frantic air. There is also her strident overprotectiveness toward Joseph.

Occasionally we get tantalizing glimpses of a woman whose resources of strength and courage are often stretched to the breaking point beneath her mask of insouciance. Her reminiscences as she bathes Joseph's infected arm crack her fortitude for a moment. She recalls when she was a beautiful girl of shining innocence, with long blond hair and "expensive long-gone dresses"; she thinks of the men she rejected; and she begins "a muffled heavy-nosed cry right into Joseph's arm basin." "I can't help it," she apologizes. "Your mother's a real person and she's got feelings. I look at what I've got now sometimes and I get sick" (121).

We learn, while following her debacle with the retired naval commander ("From the second he saw your mother there was only one thing on his mind. He saw your mother's form. . . ." [181]), that the dark despair and the uncomplaining endurance of a woman prone to the usual female fears and disorders lurk beneath her strident sexuality. "Years back," Joseph remembers, "she had gone without fuss one morning to have a fistlike growth taken from her by surgeons. It had turned out to have a long threadlike connection that ran along the side of her, making the operation a long and major one." Where the threatening "fistlike growth" had failed to destroy her self-control, the naval commander's predatory insults succeed. In a taxi she gives way to "great heaving fat-nosed whulps" (180).

Yet, the complex conception suggested by these details never coalesces into a meaningful study of a mid-century, Jewish-American woman, of a new Hedda Gabbler, blessed with energy but also afflicted with the peculiar stresses that each age fashions to hobble and control that energy. Friedman draws back from any close look through the dark glass that obscures the ache of Meg's life. Instead, he burlesques her grief: "She went into a wide-nostriled, mascara-tinted series of whulps, drawing her lips back over teeth that had had much bridgework done on them." The momentary Black Humor focus on today's woman blurs into the seriocomic view that an embarrassed boy has of a flamboyant mother who he wished "had a neater, more conservative way" of crying (182).

Friedman plays Meg for laughs. He endows her with *chutzpah* or gall that puts to nought the daily disappointments of life in a three-room Brooklyn flat. Meg the Borscht-circuit queen, a hybrid of Catskill matron and Bleeker Street Auntie Mame, predominates in her portrait. She ostentatiously overtips; she passes out pairs of lady's gloves to airline stewardesses; and she gyrates slowly to dance music down the aisle of an airliner. She breezes into crowded theaters and restaurants, past long queues, brassy and resourceful, her mouth minty fresh and her bosom exhaling clouds of perfume. A wisecrack forever on her lips, she banters, sweetly tough, with doctors, taxi drivers, bartenders, bellhops, waiters, cleaning women, sales clerks, and neighbors. She is the embattled matriarch fending off chiselers and bullies; the worldly-wise New Yorker battling daily against high fees and inflated prices; the harassed mother indulging her smart-aleck, back-talking son; the sentimental Jew drooling over honeycake and youthful rabbis.

She has a touch of the misfortune-prone *schlimazl*, with the contrary genius of the professional fund-raising *schnorrer* or beggar, to ingratiate her with everyone. She calls the police when Joseph stays out late on a date, and, nightgown clad, tours the town in a squad car in search of him. To the grinning delight of the patrolmen, she has to be slid farcically, hair disheveled, and stockings all "scuffed and domelike blisters" (279–80), through the window because the car doors are stuck. She talks in an exaggerated English rendering of Yiddish syntax. "I'll tell you what, sweetheart," she finally concedes to Joseph. "As long as you're capable of having a new kind of mouth that I'd give a nickel to know who supplied you with it, tomorrow morning I'll quietly pack my bag and buy a ticket and you won't even know I'm gone" (272). And in a long speech that is one part Molly Bloom and two parts Molly Goldberg, in which she lists all the reasons why she should hasten back to New York City, the participial clause of the Yiddish sentence becomes a litany of urban Jewish middle-class triumphs and tribulations (280–82).

This speech of Meg's epitomizes the divided intentions inherent in the conception of her character. In her opening statements, when she itemizes the problems she faces daily as a mother and a housewife, they read like the eternal bill of complaints of the female: a husband who is "a helpless imbecile," an apartment which needs painting, a headstrong daughter who is bent on a bad marriage, local charities that demand her time—the archetypal cry of James Joyce's Anna Plurabelle transliterated into the humdrum strains of a Bensonhurst *hausfrau*. Midway in her soliloquy, however, her lament turns from rue and pathos to braggadocio. She becomes a *soubrette* in a comedy routine, a petticoated *miles gloriosus* or braggart combattant jousting with city hall, a bra-and-girdled Ziegfield plucking future stars out of chorus lines. "There isn't a judge—we'll forget what's on his mind for the moment—who wants to set me up in politics," she outrageously claims, "that if I let him you'd never see me standing in supermarkets like Mrs. Saltzman, the very important district attorney's wife, to save three cents on a can of string beans?" Her fancy careens onward like a runaway train. "There aren't fortytwo positions on Broadway that I would step into with how I forgot more about the theater than J. J. Shubert ever knew?"

She tops this claim about show-business know-how with four more "O altitudos" before winding down to a Biedermeier bourgeois complaint about the career woman: "I don't have fourteen offers a day to sit like a madonna and play mah-jongg if I wanted to be the kind that doesn't care if their families croak as long as they've got their pleasure? And if their husbands get a hardboiled egg for dinner that night, that's all right, too? Sometimes I wonder who's better off, the other kind that sits and is smug and says to the world, 'All right, entertain me' or your mother with the way she's constructed and how she could love that it's not even healthy" (281–82).

In this soliloquy of Meg's, Friedman displays both the strengths and the weaknesses of his sensibility. He is acutely responsive to the subterranean emotions of the *kleine mensch* or little man and to the pent-up frustrations of twentieth-century urban existence, and his ability to invent situations dramatizing these insights is equal to his perceptions. Yet, as Coleridge was fond of remarking, a man's virtues can also be the genesis of his faults; and Friedman's imaginative fecundity, ordinarily an artistic asset, often becomes a liability when not rigorously controlled—when he allows his witty fancy to take over and invents one marvelous absurdity after another, as in the second half of Meg's complaint. Verbal facility has then displaced profound psychological perception, and farcical anecdote has replaced moving social commentary.

The obvious explanation of Friedman's reticence—that Meg perilously approximates the character of Friedman's mother [4]—is unconvincing. For one, while Friedman has a fixation on the Meg type (she appears essentially unchanged in *Stern, A Mother's Kisses*, and *Scuba Duba*), the absence of serious psychological treatment of any woman in his stories persuasively points to Friedman's difficulty in projecting himself into the female mind. He recognizes this narrowness in his fictional talents, admitting that so far he has felt confident only when handling either a masculine or a "flip-chick" point of view.[5]

Then there is Friedman's fictional use of stereotypes as a method of emphasizing the abstract and conformist tendencies of our technological society. Indeed, most of his characters even lack names: they are simply sisters, grandmothers, college girls, gangland girl friends, and adolescents—types which Friedman daringly uses as the basis of his characterizations, adding details which transform the type into a recognizable product of his imagination. He has followed this procedure, in part at least, with Meg. As Friedman passionately insists,[6] she is no exact stereotype of the Jewish mother; for her free-wheeling, uninhibited sexuality represents a radical departure from the conventions.[7] In addition, she has a distinctive vitality and verve. She also is not unaware of her Jewish manner, so that her outrageous conduct is often a put-on, at times self-mocking in its honesty. She has one foot in the "matzo-ball world," to quote Friedman, and the other foot in the American contemporary scene.[8]

Still, no amount of critical theorizing can wholly explain away our sense that vital links have been left out of Meg's portrait. As his own view of her indicates, Friedman ultimately begs the question of what ails Meg. Instead of the profound psychological exploration that the conception of Meg demands, we are asked to accept a skillful variation on the conventional Jewish mother.

Meg's overprotectiveness more often than not becomes indistinguishable from the comical solicitude of the stereotype mother of Yiddish literature. Like Salinger's Bessie Glass, who also shows symptoms of psychic malaise that is left undiagnosed, Meg is not even spared the ubiquitous all-weather cure-all of Jewish mothers, the "holy bowl of soup" (as Zooey sardonically calls it) bubbling on the kitchen stove and thrust everlastingly at her suffering children.

V *Form and Content*

A Mother's Kisses is about a boy's growing up. Not without trauma, Joseph progresses from a son's acquaintance with his mother and sister's girdles to an adolescent's knowledge of girls' "intricately webbed, circulation-pinching foundation garments." His explorations never get much beyond the stage of timid probes, as in the instance of his date with a "slow-witted farm girl" whose sorority sisters had encased her responsive "plump backwoods body" protectively in a "network of heavy, powerfully seamed contraptions" of garments. Over these "metallic dainties" Joseph hacked and pried for hours without success, other than jimmying loose "one dull sliver of upper back" (277–78). Moreover, his other forays into female territory remain innocent enough: he exchanges an innuendo in mock shyness with a strange co-ed; he dances with a girl whose behind is "Lindy-hop hardened"; and he sunbathes on the roof of his apartment building with an older girl, who has a reputation of being fast and who lowers her halter straps sophisticatedly and gives him leads on what to expect in freshman Beowulf lectures. He dances with a reputedly sexy French teen-ager and succeeds in stealing five minutes of heavy petting from another girl. Less innocent, although not wholly to his undeveloped tastes, is his share in the bathing of a girl by a neighborhood gang. For the most part, Joseph's erotic activities are marked by constant longing and considerable frustration.

Joseph's universe is composed of timid peeks into an incomprehensible, fragmented world that is inhibiting. For him the relatedness of actions, the cause and effect of events, remains an article of faith of adults that he must take on trust. The *sine qua non* of this view is expressed by Joseph when, suffering from an infected arm, he feels morosely that "the whole germ theory of disease was a hoax . . . and that when people got better it was by wild coincidence" (126). Nor is Joseph's suspicion of a crack in the world's logic allayed by his family's inexplicable psychosomatic illnesses, or by their other inspired absurdities such as his father's patois of irrelevant commonplaces and his sister's inappropriate displays of pulchitrude.

The formal structure of the Friedman novel reflects this metaphysics of the absurd. The reasons behind human actions are complex and ultimately defy analysis, and it is wise to hold as suspect any neat formulation of them. Only *what* a person does or says is above suspicion. Under the circumstances, the full documentation of the Naturalistic novel is irrelevant; the Existential reaction to each divisive moment becomes the only reality. In aping the episodic logic of Existential existence, Friedman takes great risks. He parallels the absence of congruity in Joseph's world with a narrative that ignores, for the most part, all but the rudiments of family background, place and time, and plot development. Friedman, of course, suggests that there are deeply rooted sociosexual origins to the reactions of his fictional characters; but he is careful to leave them implicit and imprecisely defined. The concentration of the narrative on the surface of events skillfully masks his scrutiny of human motives.

Such an esthetic places heavy responsibility on the language to convey more than the explicit statement of the story. Consequently, Friedman is highly conscious of his prose style, relying on it to limn the narrative with a chiaroscuro of those intuitions of his which give psychological basis to the actions of his characters. He has fashioned a prose sensitive to the nuances and the inanities of ordinary talk; yet no one speaks quite like his fictional creations do. In this sense, Friedman writes a prose as idiosyncratic and as suggestive of the felt life as that of Henry James or of William Faulkner—a prose nervously responsive to both the stereophonic-stroboscopic scene and to the dark totemic surges of our blood and the dark satanic mills of the mind.

CHAPTER *4*

The Short Stories

BRUCE JAY FRIEDMAN has written to date over fifty short stories. The earliest, "The Man They Threw Out of Jets," was completed toward the end of his stint at the age of twenty-three or twenty-four in the United States Air Force. A slice-of-life rendering of the jet-gunnery ranges of an Air Force base in Arizona, where a vintage major who dates back to prop planes carries on a one-man guerrilla resistance to the creeping encroachment of jets by refusing to fly them, the narrative is handled conventionally but with considerable skill for a first story. The device of using the point of view of a dismayed young service photographer, who is on the base for one day to take pictures of the gunnery range, provides an objective contrast to the vehemence of the major's sensibility. Despite its conventionality, the story foreshadows the direction that Friedman's fiction eventually took. The flip diction avoids any jarring lapses in taste, while striking the ear as brilliantly contemporary. Such diction also figures in the major's bombastic talk, as in his first words to the young photographer:

> "What are you? A first or second balloon? . . .
> "First lieutenant," I said.
> "First balloon," he said. "All right, first balloon. You're a first balloon, you been around long enough to know today's pay day. I got 150 bastardos waiting out there to be paid." (*City Class,* 148) [1]

The surrealistically improbable occurs when the flap of the rear baggage compartment of the major's beloved T-6 single prop comes off in the hand of the lieutenant as he prepares to climb in. "You broke my plane," the major laments in a litany of repetition, "Why did you break my plane? . . . Get in my plane . . .

Get off the ground and get in my plane. You broke my god-damned plane, now get in. *Get in!*" (149). The instinctive way in which the major flies the plane in sickening lurches as if it were an extension of his own lunging body becomes ultimately for the wondering lieutenant the index of sanity in an otherwise insane jet world. The major "was really important and very sane," the lieutenant decides, and "everyone else was crazy" (159).

Friedman is attempting in this story the difficult imaginative task of reversing our usual perspective on events and of forcing us to accept the bizarrely quixotic as the normal. By the conclusion, reality, if not exactly changing places with fantasy, has had cast upon it sufficient feelings of the fantastic to make the whole notion of normality debatable. Thus, in Friedman's first successful essay at storytelling, Friedman exhibits the integrated sensibility which matures steadily with little radical change into the free-wheeling Black Humor of *Stern, A Mother's Kisses, Scuba Duba,* and the short stories of *Black Angels.* In them, he details so many symptoms of disquiet in contemporary manners that normality's clean bill of health seems to have developed a perpetual cough and squint.

Friedman's first story to be published, "Wonderful Golden Rule Days," appeared in the October 31, 1953, issue of the *The New Yorker.* It satirizes the nostalgia of adults, who sentimentalize the nightmare of adolescent school days into the rosy haze of Eugene O'Neill's *Ah Wilderness.* Again the form demonstrates firm control but little experimentation. After a pedestrian roll call of hated classes from the mornings' first to the afternoon's last of a four-teen-year-old boy, the story narrates how he came to dislike his last class, woodworking, even more violently than all his other courses. The story is interesting, primarily, for the first appearance of a dominant motif in Friedman's fiction: the helpless, nightmarish terror felt by the Milquetoasts of a technological bureaucracy who are trapped in a social situation which they are powerless to control.

The acceptance by *The New Yorker* of his second try at short story writing catapulted Friedman into the company of Jean Stafford, Rebecca West, S. J. Perelman, James Thurber, Peter De Vries, J. F. Powers, Irwin Shaw, and Raold Dahl, to mention some of the writers appearing that year between the covers of one of the most prestigious magazines of the day for a writer.

This success made him temporarily a hero among his underground New York writer friends. Recalling this heady experience, Friedman believes now that his instant success was the worst thing that could have happened to him. It lured him into writing Realistic mood sketches, "flat autobiographical snips," as Friedman was later to call them,[2] which are the hallmark of *The New Yorker* style—into writing stories at first that are at variance with the direction his fiction eventually took. The earliest of these stories include, besides "Wonderful Golden Rule Days," "The Trip" and "The Good Time," both early versions of the mother-son entanglement later reworked into the Meg-Joseph story of *A Mother's Kisses*.

The stories were mostly, as Friedman admits today, pieces of novels. Since such stories failed to hold his interest very long, he quickly tired of the type of narrative which did not allow him to explore our flip-out, pop responses to the grotesque mid-twentieth-century world of conglomerates, electronic gadgetry (with trip tickets to the moon already being booked), organization men, and random atavistic savagery. In the mid-1950's, he spent three years of concentrated writing on a picaresque army tale in the *Catch-22* vein. Tentatively titled "You Are Your Own Hors D'Oeuvres," the novel failed to hold together and remains unpublished. He then returned in the late 1950's to the short story, but now he tried to write contrived fantasies of the sort written by John Collier and Raold Dahl in an effort to break out of the naturalistic mold. With these stories, he finally found his métier; and writing at great speed, he completed in about eight months in 1958 most of the stories subsequently collected in *Far from the City of Class*. By 1960 Friedman felt that he had mastered the art of storytelling sufficiently to attempt a second novel. Using some of the hallucinatory technical effects learned from writing the short stories, he finished *Stern* in less than an year in 1961. With its publication, he became clearly identified with such Black Humorists and social critics as Louis-Ferdinand Céline, John Barth, and Terry Southern with whom he feels a temperamental and literary kinship.

In the 1960's, despite his increasing preoccupation with the novel and the theater, Friedman continued to write prolifically in the short-story form. For the most part, he looks upon this writing as a necessary financial chore and disclaims any lasting literary value for it. He is aware of its limitations, its one-dimensional treatment of character, in comparison to the greater scope of the novels. He admits that he relies on narrative twists—on juxtapositions of psychological and emotional quirks with social and economic patterns of behavior—as, for example, in "The Investor," where a hospital patient's temperature reflects the market fluctuations of a glamor stock. Friedman delights in the writer's craft of capping such a witty commentary on the participatory interrelation of the human and nonhuman appurtenances of our lives with a surprise ending that incredibly goes the original situation one better. The medical specialist who correctly diagnoses the puzzling case soon discovers that his sexual activity with a new wife—the widow of a market-fever victim—is also locked into the movements of another stock.

Despite Friedman's disclaimers about the importance of his short fiction, his stories provide him with a proving ground for his ideas. In writing the short story he learned how to transmute his private experiences into public commentary, and he felt his way into the characters and situations of *Stern* and *A Mother's Kisses*. In the best of these stories, as in his novels and play, the social and the psychological levels merge into a profound commentary on the sexual fears and corporation speculations of the mid-century American. Thus, Friedman connects the postwar fever to "make a killing" in the stock market in "The Investor" with our erotic impulse. Our obsession with records—with graphs, time-motion studies, and cost analysis—which document the free-enterprise system nicely camouflage our fears of either impotence or satyriasis.

One of the root causes of physical illness is thus pinpointed in the economic fever chart of the nation. In a sense, "The Investor" is a refinement on the slogan, "As General Motors goes, so goes the country." And our sneaking admiration for satyriasis is made explicit in the surprise conclusion. The feverish patient had neglected his wife of "voluptuous figure," frequenting the burlesque instead; eventually, he succumbs to a body temperature of 52⅞, brought on by a two for one split of Plimptons stock. His doctor, smitten by his widow's "big boobs," marries her; and with sexual fervor he pounces on her twice daily during their one-week honeymoon. By "the eighth day of their marriage, the specialist found himself tearing home in mid-afternoon to institute a third, between hospital research and afternoon clinic," but when the couple began to indulge in five, with the doctor canceling afternoon clinic, they realized, "at first in panic and then with mounting satisfaction, that they were on a new issue, something called Electronic Lunch, which had come on the big board almost unnoticed but seemed to be climbing swiftly thanks to recommendations from two old-line investment services" (*Black Angels*, 48).

For the most part, Friedman's short stories have been a commerical success—which may influence his opinion of them. His initial publication in *The New Yorker* was a harbinger of the future, for in the 1960's, he had regularly contributed stories, as well as journalistic pieces, to *Cavalier, Esquire, Playboy,* and the *Saturday Evening Post*. To date, he has gathered thirty-two of these stories into two collections, *Far from the City of Class* (1963) and *Black Angels* (1966).

I   Far from the City of Class

The sixteen stories of *Far from the City of Class* divide unevenly into those based on Friedman's four student years at a Midwestern university, those on two nonflying years in the United States Air Force, and those which reach out past the boundaries of our senses for a vantage point from which to look back squint-eyed at our culture. The first grouping, naturally the largest, contains Friedman's initial efforts at fiction, all written in his early Realistic vein. Besides "The Man They Threw Out of Jets" and "Wonderful Golden Rule Days" (which reaches back to Friedman's high school days), there are the title story, "Far from the City of Class," "The Trip," "The Subversive," "The Good Time," and "The Canning of Mother Dean."

"Far from the City of Class" and "The Subversive" are variations on the same basic situation: the visit of an Easterner to the home of a Midwesterner who has befriended him. In the title story the two Easterners, Hank, an aggressive city-slicker from Newark, and the unnamed narrator, a mild boy from New York City, are college students in a dull Midwestern college town. They are invited to spend the weekend of the mid-semester recess at the home of a fellow student, Butz, whose father owns a grocery store in Kansas City. Called Save-A-Dime, the store epitomizes the pugnaciously defensive, grubbing attitude of Butz's parents, who expect their son's guests to work for their room and board by delivering groceries.

The story is interesting mainly as an early study for the character of Gatesy in *A Mother's Kisses*—and as a measure of Friedman's subsequent growth as a writer, particularly in the capacity of his narrative, despite its intrinsic economy, to match an increasingly dense and complex psychology as he taps ever more surely the roots of his own psychic life. In the first version, he is content to exploit a simple contrast between big-city boys and small-town yokels. Hank's endless talk of his man-about-town reputation in Gotham is presented to us as true. Only a hint here and there suggests that his claims of being an operator are suspect: he actually lives in Newark, his scorn for "Cornville, U.S.A., home of cornballs who've never heard of Gotham" (27), is excessive; and his concern for "class" is criticized by Butz as "that New York routine" (27). Still, Hank does operate like a big-city slicker with a dumb, show-struck girl with whom Butz arranges a meeting; and Butz and his parents are laughed at as deficient in sensibility.

Using the grocery truck on their Saturday night on the town, Butz is lampooned as an insecure driver who sweats incessantly; he "gripped the wheel so tight the veins on his hands bulged out," and he drove with "his shoulders hunched way over . . . his eyes popping out nervously at the road" (27). His routine of clutching, braking, wheel-spinning, and windshield wiping becomes a humorous leitmotif for the Kansas City boy.

In the later novel version, the Times Square bravado of Hank has been deepened into a psychological study of the blow-hard little man. Like Hank, Gatesy attaches himself to a real New Yorker, whom he calls "Boss"; and spiels endlessly about how he zeros in on the Kansas Land Grant Agricultural cornball broads with the line that he is "a fabulous garment tycoon" who never walks if he can take a cab. Actually, his parents slave in a children's ready-to-wear clothing store in Philadelphia; and he proves to be ineffectual on the one occasion when he and Joseph look for girls. He is a devastating portrait of the sexually insecure youth, who substitutes fantasy for action: he talks vulgarly about his legendary potency; peoples his harem-sized, make-believe world of words with appeased females; but is paralyzed into inaction when confronted with one flesh-and-blood girl.

"The Subversive" places the East-West encounter in a military service setting. The narrator from Brooklyn meets Ed Stamm, a Midwesterner, while both are waiting for air-force assignment: the narrator, for a nonflying position ("something small and inconspicuous where my general lack of military knowhow would do the least amount of damage," [87]); Ed Stamm, for jet-fighter training. To the Brooklyn boy's flip eyes, Stamm appears to be the most All-American person he has ever met—small Iowa home town, kid sister with freckles, part-time job at a gasoline station while attending the local college, four-letter man in athletics, and for His-Girl-Back-Home, the bank president's daughter, voted "Prettiest" in her senior class—until he spends a weekend in Stamm's home. While at the dinner table on the second night, Stamm's mother, a shriveled woman with withered legs and deep crevices in her face, wheels unannounced into the room. At her appearance, Stamm stands and screams in a monotone, "SON OF A BITCH. GET IT OUT OF HERE. DIRTY. DIRTY. SON OF A BITCH. OH, DIRTY, DIRTY BITCH" (94). In one moment of horrifying disclosure, the narrator's illusions about paradise and its inhabitants are dispelled. With considerable economy of means, Friedman uncovers to our eyes the hideous lie, the emptiness, in our nostalgic faith in corn-fed, small-town America. The shock of recognition is not unlike that felt at the discovery of the demented wife in Charlotte Bronte's *Jane Eyre*, although each author exploits the revelation in his story for different ends, and Friedman secures the greater psychological advantage.

Only an unreconstructed urbanite could have written these two stories which implacably reflect Friedman's New York City background, a bias that links him to many of the other Black Humorists, particularly Thomas Pynchon. "The Canning of Mother Dean" is bent on disillusioning us of another truism: our treasured college tradition of the sweet, self-sacrificing fraternity housemother. Despite the sentimental objections of most of the fraternity, two cost-analysis-conscious members manage to get Mother Dean fired by demonstrating how her inefficiency and everyone's craving for "pointless ceremony" during the previous twenty-five years had cost the fraternity thousands of dollars. Maudlin over their dismissal of Mother Dean, the fraternity brothers mope about for a year, losing all enthusiasm for collegiate and interfraternity affairs—only to glimpse at the Summer-Queen parade not the heartbroken little old lady, whom they remember, who wore glasses, crocheted endlessly, and always wore a shawl, but a tall, erect woman with purple-tinted hair and "an almost indecently high angle to her bosom" (208). Perched in the back seat of one of the parade cars and seated beside a dark-haired middle-aged man "with a ring on his finger that glinted in the sun," she grandly waved a parade banner.

The application of systems analysis to all human activities, even those hitherto protected from such ruthless, unsentimental scrutiny, is a dogma of the 1960's. Friedman irreverently applies its assumptions in the daily operation of a fraternity as much to question its uncritically accepted dogmatism as to poke fun at the sacred traditions of college life. The incongruous combination, based on the relentless logic of a computerized culture, is an essential morpheme of Friedman's fictional language.

Another is the recurrence in his stories of an irritable, ineffectual, self-conscious youth who is not unlike Joseph in *A Mother's Kisses*. If, as William Wordsworth contended, the child is father to the man, this youth is clearly the adolescent father to Stern. He appears in two early stories, "The Trip" and "The Good Time." Equally important to the mythology of Friedman's fiction is a wise-cracking, sexually vital Jewish woman, who also makes her early appearance in these two stories. In them, however, she is only a crude approximation to Meg whose hunger for life contains an alleviating undercurrent of sad self-deprecating wisdom; whereas in the two early stories the emphasis is on the woman's vulgarity, drunkenness, promiscuity, and heavy-handed emotional involvement with her son. Similarly, the situation of "The Trip" is a shorthand version of the more sympathetic and psychologically mature treatment in *A Mother's Kisses* of Meg's trip with Joseph to college. In a third story, "The Little Ball," dealing with an ulcer patient in a hospital, Friedman draws a tense character whose nerve ends are open and raw ("when a nurse walked by he grabbed her arm and said . . . 'I'm very upset. I can feel myself going and I'd better talk to someone,'" 101)—which is an early study of Stern.

The most important stories in *Far from the City of Class*—because they point the direction which Friedman's maturing vision

was to take in the late 1950's and which was to continue to
follow through the 1960's—conjure up "a dark world of supernatural 'deals,' fixes, and forbidden allurements" [3] that masquerade in all the guises and appurtenances of our consumer culture.
The new trinity is organization, cost control, and merchandising.
However, there is a dark underside to this Madison Avenue paradise of television sponsors, product endorsements, marketing
research, packaged foods, and automatic obsolescence. Friedman
bears nervous testimony to the holiday weekend traffic statistics,
ulcers, and psychoanalysis that also figure in the corporate structure of our civilization.

In Friedman's world, as Samuel I. Bellman has aptly remarked,
a *quid pro quo* rule prevails.[4] As *kleinen menschen,* little ordinary
men, with few ennobling traits, Friedman's protagonists are
stretched on the rack of such a world. Avid to profit from the
slick giveaways dreamt up by public-relations men, they are
continually beset with anxiety and hostility when the schemes
to which they have devoted themselves prove less than perfect—
indeed, prove to be full of unspecified loopholes for the un-
designated Party of the First Part. The stories which explore this
consumer's Alice-in-Wonderland are "A Foot in the Door," "The
Big Six," "For Your Viewing Entertainment," and "Yes, We Have
No Ritchard."

"A Foot in the Door" lampoons the hopes and anticipations,
the extra dividends, upon which our insurance-regulated society
depends. A short-of-breath insurance agent named Merz (the
approximation to the French word *merde* is intentional) offers
with each cheap thousand-dollar policy a special bonus: the
realization of a material desire of the customer's. In this manner,
a Mr. Gordon acquires a house in Tall Hills, wall-to-wall carpet-
ing, membership in the Tall Hills Golf Club, elimination of his
competitor for the next senior promotion at the office, a voluptuous weekend mistress, and enough unearned income to be able
to ignore the world. The catch is that he must give something
in return. So long as he is asked to "sacrifice" someone else,
usually a relative, he is agreeable to the arrangement. As part of
the packaged deal, his Uncle Lester dies, his second baby is born
with a slightly bent nose, his nearsighted father-in-law is trans-
ferred to a new job that sends the elderly gentleman driving
along precipitous mountain passes in southern Wyoming, and his

mother is afflicted with a permanent toe fungus. When he has to lose his own hair, Mr. Gordon begins to find the conditions of the verbal agreement too sharp. And, when he has to share his wife with Merz, he wants to end the agreement. But Merz won't yield. "I took asthma, a bleeding ulcer and let a Long Island train wreck have six of my grandchildren for your wife," he explains to Mr. Gordon. "It was under a special incentive plan for us employees" (85–86).

In "The Big Six" a food company, which does not advertise, offers consumers of canned broccoli the chance "to go back and consummate early seductions that went awry" (187). A Mr. Lorsy, who has spent a lot of sleepless, thrashing nights because of his sexual maladroitness, leaps at this offer, only to find that he takes no joy in his conquests because they were not of his doing. "The whole thing was rigged by the company. All I had to do was swallow a clump [of broccoli] and go through the motions. Any idiot could have made out" (194). The only seduction that he remembers fondly is the one he consummated by himself with a girl nicknamed Any-Hour-Andrea. When he catches the company representative assigned to him moonlighting on a spare-time job, he angrily threatens to report the man. Immediately, Lorsy is whisked to the scene of his one sexual triumph. He is eager to prove himself again; but Andrea now resists his advances. "I shop at the same supermarket you do," she informs him. "You're consummating yours? Well, I'm going back, and undoing all of mine" (195).

"For Your Viewing Entertainment" satirizes the amoral control over our lives of television by suggesting that heavenly judgment is handled now through the occult world of the electronics medium and its dog-eat-dog race for prime time, sponsors, and ratings. Limbo becomes a late-night show "on sustaining," where newly deceased are given one week as master of ceremonies with a limited budget to find a heavenly sponsor by frightening to death a television viewer.

"Yes, We Have No Ritchard" laughs at the black-and-white world of Hollywood "pie-in-the-sky" plots, which we have allowed to substitute more or less for our real world. A Mr. Dalton, bred on E. G. Marshall and Cyril Ritchard productions, insists, when he finds himself in the next world, that filmland dispensation of justice be operative. Unhappy at finding that good and bad people are crowded willy-nilly into the same place, Dalton is not content until he finds some difference, however slight, in living arrangements. To his satisfaction, he unearths the fact that he wears Vic Tanny's Gym and Health Club sandals, whereas a Mr. Sydel, whom he knew in life as a crook, wears Al Roon's Athletic Club sandals.

Friedman delights in demonstrating how our viewing entertainment shapes our lives and influences our thoughts, but he has a darker view of the media than has Marshall McLuhan. Friedman takes perverse pleasure in disclosing how frequently wrong the electronic-and-screenland rendering of life can be. As with "Yes, We Have No Ritchard," the plot of "23 Pat O'Brien Movies" turns on a denial of our usual assumptions. It pits a would-be suicide against a rescue-bent policeman on the sixteenth-story ledge of a hotel. Officer Goldman is likened by the cynical suicide to the tough-talking, heart-of-gold patrolmen in Pat O'Brien movies. We learn from the ensuing conversation between the two, however, that the policeman has little more reason for living than the young man he has climbed out on the ledge to save. After each has confided to the other the joylessness of his life, the policeman without a word, not even a good-bye, executes "a perfect swan dive" off the ledge, thereby leaving the suicide-prone young man still clinging to the side of the building, asking himself, "what the hell do I do now?" (217).

Two other tales, "When You're Excused You're Excused" and "Mr. Prinzo's Breakthrough," are notable mainly for Friedman's ability to concoct stories out of such unpromising material as a commonplace utterance pushed to its logical extreme. Mr. Kessler, one of Friedman's typical compulsive types, is a Jew excused for reasons of health from attending synagogue so he can take his regular workout at the gymnasium. If the excuse works for the sabbath, Mr. Kessler reasons, it must work also for Yom Kippur, adultery, orgies, and eating ham. But he angrily draws the line at the failure of a companion to know the name of a Jewish ballplayer. "NO SON OF A BITCH IS GOING TO SAY ANYTHING ABOUT POOR 'PHUMBLIN' PHIL' WEINTRAUB ON YOM KIPPUR," Mr. Kessler screams. "I may have been excused . . . but I wasn't that excused" (57).

In "Mr. Prinzo's Breakthrough," Mr. Prinzo, in his seventh year of psychoanalysis, remains cringingly insecure, fearful even that

his analyst will disclose his confessions. Trying for a breakthrough, he exacts a solemn promise from his doctor that their
"compact . . . is pure and sacred. . . . *Your* life. *Your* welfare.
Whatever's best for *you, my* patient. That's the rule . . . all of us
go right down the line with" (111–12). Prinzo puts these assurances to the ultimate test by killing the analyst's wife and
then enlisting the man's aid not only in disposing of the body
but also in getting him out of the country. To every murmur of
protest from his analyst, he answers, "I'm your patient and the
only thing in the world that counts is how I feel" (122).

Friedman's stories shock our imagination into recognition of
the peculiar warped forms that human fidelity takes in the conformist milieu of a pop culture. The vitality of the prose, its
pulsing rock rhythms and "hip" diction, underscores his vision of
the brassy, acrid tone of the 1960's with its weird amalgam of
fin de siècle Art Nouveau and 1930's social bitterness. Friedman's
brash slanginess, often his inspired invention, conveys its own
special integrity, as in the talk of the masseur in "When You're
Excused You're Excused": " 'If I had the towel concession, I'd
have it made,' said the masseur, oiling up Mr. Kessler's body.
'You can't make it on rubs alone. You got to have rubs and
rags' " (48).

Such "brilliantly insipid dialogue" [5] creates its own inviolable
world, one that contains recognizable tags and ends of our speech
but that is also arranged in oddly new patterns at once familiar
and strange. Such is the sales patter of Mr. Merz in "A Foot in
the Door" in its combination of the secondhand car dealer's sales
pitch, the television announcer's giveaway unction, the insurance
man's moral tone, and the visitor from another planet's other-
worldliness: "I've got something else you'll want," Mr. Merz
promises Mr. Gordon after selling him a thousand-dollar endow-
ment:

> "It's a way for you to have anything in the world. I haven't
> figured out whether it's insurance or not, but I have it for you and
> we can start it off tonight. . . .
> "There'll be no nonsense and no fooling around. . . . What you
> really want is a home in Tall Hills, and one thing you'd better
> learn is that it's a waste of time to be coy on this thing. Now I
> can get it for you. What we do is make a bargain. Some of them

are going to sound strange, but they're made up that way and, frankly, I don't make them up. . . .

"All right then, now listen. . . . I don't do any paper work on these so remember it and don't come around to me and say you don't get what you were supposed to. Tall Hills is yours, if . . . Let me rephrase that. When you don't use paper work, you've got to get them straight in the talking. A *house* in Tall Hills is yours, but your baby will have to be born with a slightly bent nose. I know that you, your wife and your little girl have straight ones, but that's the way these things are made up. Sometimes a real winner comes along, but most are on this order. . . .

"Can we close? . . . It isn't that I go off and sell others when I'm finished with you. There aren't any others. I'm just tired and I get colds when I'm out late." (71–73)

Contributing to the self-sufficiency of the fictional world of Friedman is the tendency of his characters to carry on both sides of a conversation; they answer their own questions. Thus, we learn in "23 Pat O'Brien Movies" most of the routines, the tricks of the trade, designed to change the minds of would-be suicides, not from the patrolman on the assignment but from the young man threatening to dive from the sixteenth-story ledge:

"All right," said the young man, "let me tell you right now, I know the whole bit. I mean the casual thing you're pulling with the head-scratching and the we're-just-two-fellows-out-here-having-a-chat routine. I've seen it in a million Pat O'Brien movies. They picked you because you're a family man and you know I have a family and that's the way to work it with me, right? First I get a cigarette to relax me, then I hear about your kids, and we go into a little life-can-be-beautiful, right? If I act real serious, then you say, 'I dare you to jump, show-off.' If you really wanted to jump, you'd have done it long ago.' Right? . . .

"Oh, you're cute. How many times have they sent you out on these? You must be the champ of the whole police department. With the kindness and the head-scratching. Give me a little life-can-be-beautiful."

"I didn't say it can be beautiful," said the patrolman, loosening his tie. "You did. Most of the time it stinks."

"Excellent con," said the young man. "Everybody takes the good with the bad, but the chickens commit suicide, right? You plunge for the concrete and all you're proving is what a coward you are, right? You really are the cutest in the business. How many Pat O'Brien movies did you sit through to pick up this jazz, twenty-three?" . . .

"I don't think you're so different," said the patrolman, looking up and studying the gray sky.

"Good move, that sky bit," said the young man. "Instead of looking down at the crowd, look up. Get his mind on onward and upward things. Sneak in a little God when he's not looking. Twenty-four straight. You must have two hundred and twenty-four straight. I don't think I'm very different either," said the young man. "I don't say I have more troubles that your last twenty-four guys. The only thing that makes me different is that I'm stepping out into the air. You can pass me kid pictures from now till kingdom come. You can get my guard up or down and you can cigarette me until you're blind, but when that buzzer rings, I'm saying goodbye to you and hello to the pavement."

"What kind of troubles?" asked the patrolman, lighting a cigarette and not looking at the young man.

"Draw him out," said the man. "Very sneakily, get him to talk about himself and then suggest that things are always darkest before the dawn. All right, save your breath. I'll draw myself out. I don't have time to wait for your Pat O'Brien routine. . . ." (209–13)

The young man talks until he unwittingly goads the patrolman into self-confession, to an admission that life stinks and then to suicide, thereby ironically reversing and turning inside out their respective roles, with which the story began.

Such language borrows very little from the prose masters of the early decades of this century and especially from those of Friedman's contemporaries most sympathetic with his vision. An authentic vehicle for Friedman's original response to the Disneyland flora and fauna that make up the combination Frontierland and Tomorrowland of the 1960's scene, it serves him as a syntax, a magic wand, for imposing meaning on the sensibility of the times. In this respect, his stories have genuine imaginative integrity; for they order human experience into a significant pattern that is not dependent (in Louis Rubin's words) for its impact on its "faithfulness to 'real life' but on the validity of its own representation." [6]

II Black Angels

Friedman's second collection of short stories, *Black Angels,* appeared in 1966. All but one of its sixteen stories had been published the preceding four years and most showed a marked improvement over those of *Far from the City of Class.* These stories in the second collection neatly divide into fantasy and realism. Friedman is basically a social critic, as indicated by his articles in *Esquire* and *The Saturday Evening Post* on such subjects as Raquel Welch and the definitive chickie, Joe Frazier in his training camp, Adam Clayton Powell on Bimini, the Philadelphia disc jockey Jerry Blavat at a dance session, and the Chicago detectives Valesares and Sullivan on a homicide case. He continued into the mid-1960's to ignore the stale cold-war horrors of the East-West confrontation, for his compulsions directed him to examine instead our more immediately felt life of platitudes, neuroses, and patented anodynes which he finds too horrible at times to contemplate other than when refracted through the Surrealistic blur of fantasy. Like his novels, the most thoughtful of these short stories have dual psychosocial tracks.

The best of the fantasies is the title story, "Black Angels." Its hero, Stefano, is a harried suburbanite; a free-lance writer of technical manuals, he has moved into a house beyond his means and, like Stern, finds the upkeep of the grounds a cyclical nightmare. On an impulse, desperate to find a gardener cheaper than his present one, Stefano checks the advertisement of a gardener named Please Try Us; and he receives a preposterously low estimate. Tingling with both guilt and glee, Stefano quickly hires Please Try Us, a quartet of stolid Negroes who work in stifling heat "in checkered shirts and heavy pants, two with fedoras impossibly balanced on the backs of their great shaved heads" (12–13). In the next two months, for ridiculously low fees and for American cheese sandwiches given them by the conscience-stricken Stefano, they clean up the yard, fertilize the beds, shave the lawns, plant new trees, paint the house with four coats, waterproof the basement, clean out the attic, sand and shellac the floors. Stefano's property shines and is now a showplace that slows down passing cars.

At this level of the story, Stefano acts out the wish fulfillment of the suburbanite who teeters anxiously between paycheck and monthly bills. But he has an even more upsetting problem than the height of his lawn: his wife has run away with an assistant director of daytime television and has taken their ten-year-old son with her. Stefano—lonely, unsuccessful in his quest for dates with young girls, weary of "Over 28" dances—is heartsore and in need of friendly counseling, if not psychoanalytic treatment. One night, over a beer, he tells a lot of his troubles to the head Negro gardener, who listens quietly and then stuns Stefano every now and then with an ambiguous, noncommittal question, like "You think you any good?" or "How long she gone?" that jolts him into a healthy re-evaluation of his situation. Pleased with the results, Stefano asks the Negro what he would charge an hour to listen to him a couple of times a week and to pose occasionally a haymaker question. The Negro's fee of four hundred dollars floors Stefano, but his need for psychological comfort is so great that he engages the handyman on the spot. The story ends with Stefano's rambles about the similarity between his wife and his mother, while the gardener settles back in a couch, pad and pencil in hand, taking notes like a professional for the remaining minutes of the hour.

The shriek in "Black Angels" at the high price of getting one human being to listen to another is a variation on the recurrent situation in Friedman's fiction of people's confronting one another physically but failing to acknowledge the other's presence orally. This situation acquires sinister overtones, like so many of Raold Dahl's stories, when Friedman portrays his people as ready to take advantage of another's weaknesses only to discover that the chance-in-a-lifetime has a *quid pro quo* rider attached to it. At the same time that "Black Angels" looks squarely at the hidden traumas of suburbia, it glances obliquely at the fraudulent industry which has become rich on suburban ills. Many of the recent fantasies uncover the emotional quicksand that lies beneath the deceptively solid surface of some of our proudest and shabbiest national fixations. The hysteria of the stock market, parodied in "The Investor," is a witty instance of this hallucinatory version of our world.

Another story, "The Hero," satirizes the public's blind worship of a hero—any hero however grotesque and however imaginary or exploited his deeds. A boy, who doglike goes for and bites all flying feet as a result of a football head injury, becomes an overnight national hero when he loses his life while clinging with a death's grip to the fleeing heel of an assassin of The Most Important Man in the Territory. The boy's vulgarian aunt (and reluctant guardian) reaps a deluge of gifts, testimonials, and money—both movable and unmovable property, to paraphrase Wemmick in Dicken's *Great Expectations*. A coarse harridan, she is identified in the eyes of the public with her nephew and is soon receiving their accolades as if she had been the hero. She is asked to comment on national and international questions, to address patriotic rallies, and to run for political office.

"The Hero" is a parody of the aftermath of the J. F. Kennedy assassination when the wife of the murdered police officer trying to apprehend Lee Harvey Oswald, reaped over a million dollars from well-meaning citizens as reward for what had been at best a negative or unsuccessful act of heroism. "The Night Boxing Ended" takes a hard look at the covert wish behind the savage words of mayhem and abuse shouted as advice to boxers from the audience. Warming up, one such heckler at a heavyweight affair graduates from screaming insults about the fighter's nationality, which delights the fight mob, to chanting "KILL THE BASTARD . . . KICK HIS BALLS, PUNCH HIS EYES OUT. KNOCK HIS HEAD OFF. KNOCK HIS HEAD OFF" (141). This instruction the other fighter obligingly follows by blasting his opponent's head into the sixth-row ringside "in the style of a baseball hit off the end of a cracked bat . . . with a certain amount of zip to it" (142). The heckler was heard to say something like "attaboy" as he slumped back in his seat.

The final macabre touch of the story is that the whole incident represents for the narrator "no big deal," merely his "saying goodbye, officially, to Uncle Roger" (142). For several years when the narrator was a boy, his uncle had taken him each Friday night to the fights. Then, when his uncle went into a hospital, he telephoned his nephew at the office twice a week. On one of these calls the nephew had been unable to talk at the time. Unfortunately, Uncle Roger "died in less than an hour," never giving "anyone a chance to say goodbye," which worried the narrator for years. Thus, the farewell to boxing becomes symbolically a wake for the uncle, a purging of grief, the ceremonial dismemberment of the scapegoat boxer giving tragic distance not only to public but also to private guilt.

"The Mission" laughs at the fetish with which we lugubriously honor the tradition of supplying the condemned man in Death Row with a last meal of his choice, even if it means chasing half way around the world for the ingredients and for the chef capable of preparing them. In this instance, the condemned man requests "Casserole of Sharpes'—grysbok tongue with mushrooms in *béchamel* sauce" (176). "The Mission," however, is not a one-cylindered sketch, with a single theme and a single twist to the narrative; instead, it is another instance of Friedman's mastery of dual-track storytelling. The Death Row context is introduced only in the final paragraph; until then, "The Mission" purports to be a parody of the screenland superman, of the tight-lipped, little-man miracle worker, popularized by Alan Ladd.

Friedman's fascination with show business provides the bases of two other fantasies, one of the best in *Black Angels*, "Brazza-ville Teen-ager," and one, "Show Biz Connections," whose central situation had already been used in the earlier story "The Big Six." "Show Biz Connections" is a not too successful attempt to update the fable of the lion and the mouse, or of Aladdin and the genie, into what could almost be the script for a Broadway musical version of how time machines should be used. As reward for pulling a thorn out of a distinguished-looking stranger's foot, Mr. Kreevy, "a shambling, Lincolnesque man," is thrown among women about to die through some disaster. His genie-benefactor thus explains the reward:

> "What I've got for you involves women, and what I've seen of those charming little ways of yours, and those socks you wear, you need this like life itself. . . . You appear to them and sud-denly they don't mind these cute little ways of yours the way they would if they met you under different circumstances. You're the last man they'll ever have a shot at. Are you getting the picture? You show up, they know it's all over and *bam*, you're all set. As soon as you finish up I whisk you out of there. *You* don't die, just them." (101)

The inevitable *quid pro quo* interrupts Mr. Kreevy's larks when he wishes to return with one of the ladies, a redheaded actress with dazzling hips. The mysterious gentleman with the thorn in his foot agrees after many threats to bring her back, but the catch is that someone must stay behind to die—and that someone is Mr. Kreevy. As African natives come for him, the oldster and the redhead "twinkle off into the sun"; and the redhead's dazzling hips provide Mr. Kreevy with his last sight on this earth. What piquancy the story has derives from the flavor of the genie-bene-factor's language, a "show-biz" patter about the "class operation" that he runs, which contrasts roguishly with his Edwardian appearance.

"Brazzaville Teen-ager," while evoking the frenzied, halluci-nated social scene of the other fantasies, explores the psycho-sexual trauma of coming of age in America, a thematic preoccu-pation of Friedman in his novels, his plays, and his many Realistic short stories. The youth Gunther—distressed by the inherent gulf that separates father and son—dreams of a death-bed scene which would unite them. In it, the older man discloses at last, man to man, the answers to all Gunther's prurient questions about his father's sexual life—"Could he still get it up at his age? What about broads. Was Mom the first he'd ever slept with? Had he ever gone to a cathouse? Which way did he like it best, straight or tricky stuff?" (78–79)—as if sexual confidence was somehow the key to their apartness. During a mysterious collapse of the old man into himself, "accordion-style, pinching off nerves" (69), Gunther grimly conceives the idea that he must "do something painful beyond belief, the most embarrassing act he could imag-ine" (71)—but only then would his dad recover. He is driven to cadge his boss, whom he deathly fears, into performing wild promotional stunts.

Gunther is, in effect, risking sacrificial self-destruction as a way of realizing a closer blood union with his father. He bullies his employer into supplying the "doo-wah, doo-wah and yeh, yeh, yeh backgrounds" at a recording session of Little Sigmund and the Flipouts. The song, "Brazzaville Teen-ager," is about a teen-ager who accompanies his mercenary soldier father to the Congo. Homesick in Brazzaville, he writes a letter to his girl in the States, nostalgically recalling how great it had been surfing and holding hands. In its lyrics and in its association with the high decibel world of hi-fi and discotheque, the song evokes in another dimension, if it does not exactly parallel, the troubled madness and adolescent yearning of Gunther's world.

When his father recovers, Gunther finds that the inalienable gulf between them has not lessened. No confidences ensue. Despite the father's near squeak with death, the two continue to address each other in the inspired language of triviality:

> "Dad," said Gunther.
> "What's that?" the old man said, whirling suddenly as though he had guessed Gunther's dirty thoughts and might throw a decrepit punch.
> "Nothing," said Gunther.
> "I thought you wanted something. For a second there it sounded like it, but what the hell, everyone's wrong sometimes. The top men in the country." (79)

The less explicitly fantastic stories often remind one of the tales of Raold Dahl. The same ill-defined smell of danger, the same distant whiff of the sinister, and the same dimly antagonistic people appear in both men's work. The transformation of the English author's tone and setting into an American voice and milieu is, however, bonafide. Whereas Dahl portrays most frequently the English upper-middle class at home and abroad, Friedman concentrates on the mass-produced product of urban America. Whereas Dahl's characters play for keeps a deadly game of get-the-other-fellow, Friedman's characters try to play the game but never quite succeed. Dahl is attracted to the story possibilities of such gadgetry and special situations as computers, wine tasting, picture restoration, and dog racing; Friedman, while intrigued by such ridiculous occupations as sectional-couch making, shoulder-pad cutting, and the myriad peripheral jobs in show business, is stung into creativity by his contemplation of human obsessions, impulses, and undefined family antagonisms. Whereas the note of evil lurking behind the surface statement of the Dahl story is Boris Karloff-like in its somber taste and impeccable manners, that of the Friedman story is closer to Jaques Tati in its anarchic camaraderie and misfired impetuosity. In three stories in *Black Angels*—"The Punch," "The Humiliation," and "The Operator"—the quintessential Friedman protagonist stumbles to a badly compromised victory in his frustrated efforts to accommodate his personal habits to those of a cultural stereotype.

The pervasive battle metaphor in *Stern* and in "The Enemy," another short story in *Black Angels,* reflects Friedman's obsessive concern for the random mayhem of contemporary life which permeates every facet of our day and scars even the traditionally sacred unit of the family. We need not recall the post-World-War-II role of America as an international policeman but only note the increasing incidence of parental injury of babies and toddlers, as reported by doctors and hospitals, to grasp the relevance of this motif in Friedman's work. The compulsion of our time to settle matters with a clean punch "on the point of the jaw, movie style" (26) is underscored by the story "The Punch." Harris, a tall and hulking but "not particularly well-muscled" (20) man, has a marriage which becomes a recurrent nightmare because his wife eagerly expects him to act like a Hollywood matinee idol by socking people in the face at the slightest provocation. Nagged by his gloomy need to prove his masculinity, he suddenly comes out of his "long Gandhi-like conciliatory period" (28) and impulsively strikes somebody for taking a cab he had hailed. In the exhilaration of his newly found *machismo,* he discovers that he has also lost his guilty dependence on his wife for approbation: "What happened, he wondered, when you smacked wives in the jaw. . . . Maybe they weren't so fragile. Some wives had hard, cold, mean little faces and could probably take a punch better than you thought. A well-timed one that missed the teeth and passed up the nose, yet got the job done just the same" (34). With this surprise twist to Harris' conjugal problem, Friedman hints at the sexual origin of much of today's random violence.

The need of Harris to return every injury with interest is retold in "The Humiliation" in words reminiscent of *Stern.* On a once-in-a-lifetime European holiday with his wife and child, and determined to enjoy the foreignness of it all, Gribitz encounters an American who had made a fool of him fifteen years before when both were in the Air Force when he had been an inexperienced shavetail; the other, a triple-hitch master sergeant. Gribitz's ability to take pleasure in the strange French experience, croissants and all, becomes impossible until he has had his revenge. "I know a little bit about myself," he confesses to the ex-sergeant; "and if I've got something like that bothering me, it can throw off my whole life. Something like a splinter. It's no bigger than a hair but you know the kind of grief it can give you. Am I getting through to you at all?" Impassively, the man lets Gribitz re-enact the humiliation, this time with the tables turned; but Gribitz derives no satisfaction from it because his tormentor fails to see that revenge has been taken. The story ends with

Gribitz still afflicted, like Stern, with doubts about himself. "I'll get you for this," he screams. "I don't care if it takes another fifteen years. You can hide in the goddamned mountains of Tibet and I'll smoke you out and beat your head till you're bloody. YOU'VE GONE AND SPOILED MY WHOLE EUROPEAN VACATION, YOU SON OF A BITCH" (188).

The postwar era of affluence and global vacations, which provides "The Humiliation" with its context, also receives attention in "The Operator." The hard work of having a good time in a strange place—sitting nightly at a sidewalk cafe, as had Gribitz and his wife, to stare across the street at people in another sidewalk cafe (178)—takes on the shabby air of the annual sexual fling in "The Operator," which satirizes the reputation of pre-Castro Havana as a sin town. When Lotito arrives in Cuba to chase the girls, he envisions himself for three days as "the center of subtle tangled relationships, all involving bored, casual, pointless Seberg-type lovemaking" (55). Following a popular guidebook on how to approach the female sex, he chases down one girl after another; but he is dispelled by one girl's bad breath, is taken for six weeks of salary vainly entertaining two others, is made love to imperfectly by one, and has his bed vomited on by yet another. Dissatisfied with the direction the evening has taken, he ends the night paying for five unsatisfactory minutes of a prostitute's time in a dump along the ocean bay. Still determined to find the Havana of barroom gossip and travel folder, he resolves to get up bright and early the next morning to "do things right and this time *really* have himself a ball" (68).

Two other stories document the sexual hallucinations of the ordinary and not so ordinary citizens of the American urban scene. "The Interview" consists of the stream of consciousness of a personnel director for a publishing house of salacious books as he interviews a job applicant. From the impersonal, sketchy facts of a vita sheet, he spins the life of a Greenwich Village chick: "Seminude parts in shoestring-budget 8-mm. films. . . . Drugs, of course, and three men in a bed, all night long, with no sex, just friendship and intimacy. Pottery course at the New School, little water-coloring on Sundays. Affair with one Negro jazz musician; on a dare, take your breasts out in a Forty-second Street film house. Great pad, roaches, little fireplace and lovemaking to *Tristan and Isolde* . . ." (93–94).

"Let Me See Faces" presents a Village Holly Golightly by way

of her smutty-minded stream of consciousness as she entertains
one of her legion of "quick bash-up boys," one of the "Eileen-I-
need-you-fast-and-violent. Monday nights and Friday lunch hour"
Mr. Finks before they rush back to Diapersville (163).

Friedman's best stories tabulate our humdrum thoughts and
actions, our daily existence, as if life were a frightening ride in
a Laugh-in-the-Dark. By a slight shift in perspective, he causes
our mundane assumptions and habits of mind suddenly to loom
gross and grotesque in our imagination. Thus, "The Enemy" is
a story about the zest with which the female members of a family
wage battle when united in a common front against interloping
in-laws. Well told from the point of view of the son who observes
his mother, aunt, and grandmother march and countermarch in
perpetual flanking actions against the wife of his uncle, the story
includes the nightmarish moment twenty years later when the
son finds that his wife is the new object of attack in the late night
phone calls of his mother.

The story contains a full gallery of Friedman characters: the
uncle who is intermittently insane but a genius in his secretive
maneuverings in the stock market, the father (or other elderly
gentleman) who utters commonplace maunderings in a porten-
tous tone of voice, the mother who gregariously carries on an
incessant guerrilla warfare with an evolving set of enemies, the
grandmother who totters senilely about muttering Hebraic
curses and hauling food to junior members of the family, the aunt
who owns a hardware store from which she annually dispenses
cut-rate bargains to the family, and the son who passively observes and endures a ubiquitous female tyranny. The caricature
of Aunt Ramona is pure Friedman in its magnification of subterranean gestures and seldom-observed details. She is described
as a very nervous "tiny, saintlike person who . . . was always
rolling up things, pieces of napkin, matchbook covers, edges of
menus, and sticking them in her ear for a quick shake. When she
used up one ear sticker, she immediately got to work on another"
(115). Friedman's fondness for this idiosyncrasy has prompted
him to give it also to Joseph's Aunt Hester, in *A Mother's Kisses,*
who always walked the twenty miles from her house to Joseph's
while "curling up little papers along the way and dropping them
into her purse for use on arrival as ear stickers" (148).

Like the Andy Warhol paintings of ubiquitous car wrecks in

his series on "Death in America," Friedman's stories document the disruptive effect on our lives of an ordinariness that has become monstrous. These stories are concerned with the insane complacence with which we accept human suffering and random violence on an industrial scale. Hence, the Friedman story is not, like so many of Franz Kafka's, or, in our own time, of William Burroughs' stories, a hallucination whose surface remains carefully discrete and dissociated from direct connection with actuality as we know it. Friedman considers such stories to be unworked dreams, the raw material which must be given a social or real application if it is to have artistic relevance. He aims to bring the dream a quarter turn back to reality. As with so many Americans in their thirties and forties, the movies have had a profound effect on his notion of what constitutes manners and culture. The cinematic focus has always tended to metamorphose reality into a Lotus land of realized dreams. Friedman has merely shifted this focus ninety degrees, so that we see both the Ford assembly line and the penthouse dream, both the unassailable girl next door and the complacent harem, not as one superimposed on the other but as one slightly askew from the other.

The discrepancy between the language and the situations of Friedman's stories underscores this blurred focus. Friedman's modern rhetoric reflects stylistically and rhythmically the "hippy's" unashamed joy in the floridity of *Art Nouveau,* his disdain for euphemisms, his submission to high-decibel rock rhythms, and his unabashed concentration on his own feelings. At the same time, the world Friedman describes is less redolent of the psychedelic 1960's than of the sentimental 1940's. His world does not yet know, or ignores, freeways, Sputnik, the California and Far West migration, the postwar baby boom, Russia, Vietnam, and the Israeli-Arab confrontation. Friedman's is still a world of fifty-dollar-a-week salaries, neighborhood soda fountains, movie stars of the early "talkies," prop-driven airplanes, vaudeville, big bands, Cuban vacations, and the first tentative moves to the suburbs. The result is a dislocation stylistically that corroborates the narrative insinuation of these stories about the breakdown of the distinction in our ordinary intercourse between reality and fantasy.

CHAPTER 5

The Dick

FRIEDMAN'S MOST recent novel *The Dick* eschews the aura of the 1940's—which so characterizes *Stern* and *A Mother's Kisses*, despite their contemporary concern with civil disorder—for an undisguised confrontation of the topical. The shift to contemporary setting and to characters with conventionally fleshed-in backgrounds, family histories and social identities, represents fictionally both a loss and a gain. On the one hand, language and situation show noticeable deterioration. Much of the nervous energy and psychological pertinacity of *Stern* has hardened into mannerism in *The Dick*. On the other hand, Friedman extends his frame of reference beyond the syndrome of the castrating mother-wife and the dominated son-husband and beyond the absurdity of the unalleviated situation of Black Humor. A "Now" generation affirmation informs the ending of this novel.

As an article he wrote in 1967 for the *Saturday Evening Post* on the daily dangers and boredom of two Chicago police detectives indicates, Friedman has been intrigued the past several years by the official aspect of the law-and-order question, just as he had been in previous years by the fears of the vulnerable citizen. In *The Dick*, he captures the social isolation of big-city policemen; their clannishness and clownish paranoia; their security-conscious adjustment, taut-jawed and gimlet-eyed, to daily existence on the periphery of the homicidal world of crime; their vulnerable families, "sitting ducks in a sea of crime-fighters" (33); [1] and their elitist isolation from the nonlaw-enforcement part of the community.

But Friedman's previous fiction has prepared us to expect him to cast a wider net than that needed for ensnaring the topic of law and order, and our expectations are not disappointed. Besides dealing with the usual range of activities at a homicide bureau, he squares off on school zoning; community integration; public-

education curriculum; relationship of the races; Birchite sentiments; real and presumed threats to personal safety in a black,
or poverty, area; and many of the sensitive aspects of the melting-
pot crisis in America. Additionally, in the problem of crime and
law enforcement resides a philosophical question of civil conformity. Here lies thematically the plimsoll line of *The Dick.*

Much has been written of late about the changing habits of the
American. No longer is he content to be born, educated, married,
and buried in Midtown, America, accepting without quarrel the
values of his community. A plurality of choices now confronts
him: the black experience, the "hippy" commune, the suburban
swinging set, the singles group, the weekend campers, the surfing
crowd—the list could go on indefinitely. If Middle America still
follows in the staid path of the "American Way," the rest of the
country now believes it can don life styles with the casual frequency that it changes clothes. Indeed, in a large measure, America's sense of self has become unfixed as it varies with the role a
person adopts as he moves from group to group. We have been
sold the belief that we may become whatever we desire: television tells us around the clock that our personality can be altered
by the simple expedient of changing the model of our car, the
tint of our hair, the brand of our mouthwash. External appearance identifies the inner man: long hair and Levis mark the
"freaks," uniform or business suit the "straights," and hot pants
the "swingers."

But all is not well in this instant paradise. Alterations in the
habits of a lifetime are not realized without trauma, as is evi-
denced by the concurrent rise of sensitivity sessions designed to
get at the essential person. Friedman has made this contemporary
"rites of passage" the particular province of his fiction.

I *The Homicide Detectives*

The protagonist of *The Dick* is an aging ("he was slipping up
on forty," [5]) public-relations man for homicide bureaus; and
his specialty is preparing boards of clippings designed to repair
the grim and tawdry images of the criminal divisions of police
departments. Born Kenneth Sussman in New York City, he is
known after seventeen years of living "in polite and hearty towns
of the Midwest" (4) as Kenneth LePeters. He has recently fol-

lowed his boss Bruno Glober back East to "a large, violent, but somehow conscience-stricken homicide bureau" (8). He has bought a house in a cordoned-off suburb which is a two-hour drive from the city and which is known as "Detectives' Hill" because it was once favored by retired police chiefs, a community made fiercely law-abiding by the ex-dicks lolling about. Only nominally a cop, since he cannot officially lay claim to being a detective, LePeters exists on the periphery of the police world; a half-sized or "baby" badge is pinned to his chest; and an empty silver holster on his desk is used to hold his pencils and glue brush.

Much of the first half of the novel occupies itself with LePeter's indoctrination into the daily routine and his introduction to the members of the bureau. He takes a homicidal psychiatry test, "designed to put the finger on queers and flush them out of the department" (13), which is administered by a psychoanalytic specialist in homicide, Doctor-Detective Worthway, who pins the classic Freudian interpretation on the bureau's obsession with guns and bullets. At the armory LePeter is issued a regulation Smith and Wesson .38; but, to his relief, he is not called upon, as he had at his last bureau, to qualify four times a year in "mad dog" shooting, "a style in which you whipped out your gun, fell to your knees, and without taking time to aim, got off volleys of crazed, yelping, animal-like shots at a human silhouette" (16). As a new man on the staff, he is the butt of some practical jokes; and one is his being tricked into an interrogation session with a suspect. Without too much difficulty, on the other hand, he falls into the bureau rhythm of endless on-duty coffee klatches and after-hour saunas where the detectives ("Tough as lead pipes around the bureau" and "whose very breath was sour with violence") seemed harmless and a little silly "in the baths, gunless, stripped down, some of them many-bellied" (33).

In Friedman's hands, the homicide officers become a rogues gallery of police types, caricatures of men for whom mayhem and death are staples of life. Chief Guster, the head of homicide, reminds LePeters of a money-lending shylock his father had dealt with during the depression. "Up to his ears in aggravated batteries" (12), the Chief dismisses LePeters with a single hissed word, "Compassion." Gibney of petty vice, feigning official duties, takes a "regular morning riffle through the sex-crime photo files," occasionally holding a picture aloft and hollering, "Here's a lulu" (13). Lieutenant Riggles of polygraph constantly straps himself to the lie detector to test the equipment, which he claims he has been unable to fool in twenty years. Detective Hortham of micro-analysis is the bureau ghoul and introduces himself to LePeters by flinging in his face a pair of evidential panties off a dead air-line stewardess; Detective Gus Flamoyan, the bureau jokester and general wise guy, intuitively penetrates LePeter's seventeen-year secret, nicknaming him Izzy. The bureau's show-Negro, Detective Medici, is assigned to the vice squad and is known as the Dean of Child Molestation; and he wears more guns than anyone in the department. And, finally, there is LePeters' assistant, Detective Teener, a legendary gunfighter who has been trimmed down in size through pieces of his body being shot away by gunfire in a shoot-out with a nine-man gang in which Teener had killed eight.

As this brief summary suggests, Friedman parodies the widespread notion that psychologically as well as fraternally law enforcer and law breaker are more alike than dissimilar—an insight full of possibilities for extended fictional treatment; but the parodic situations are too often broadly conceived. The killer instinct of the detectives is reflected satirically in the custom of each one's posting his kill record on a little corkboard inside his footlocker. Medici, to celebrate his thirteenth—"slaughtering an unarmed Mexican hophead in the back row of a movie theater as he slept"—"blew the entire bureau to delicious spareribs and thick chocolate shakes" (37). Another detective conducts a one-man campaign for the Spanish garrote as a neater way of killing than the noose, and he demonstrates nightly in front of the Coke machine with a silk handkerchief. And all the detectives pride themselves on their ability to rough up a suspect sufficiently to extract a fast confession. The legendary dumbness of the flatfoot is laughed at when an electronic system, installed to speed telephone reports of murders and incoming calls, grinds to a halt while the "baffled dicks" struggle to get "the hang of the confusing electronic callboard" (193). Inevitably, one of the "trusted, old-line dicks known for his soft, casual style around the bullpen, all in marked contrast to the savagery with which he smashed the heads of law violators," turns homicidal, "gunning down . . . a slew of fathers of teen-age kids." The incidence of the "rogue law-officer" plunges the dicks into a grim and sullen mood, as if "each detective had a horrible fear that deep in his own recesses there existed a tiny homicidal button that might one day get itself pushed" (194).

Cut from the same cloth as Stern, LePeters steps gingerly around "these folksily violent men" (283), for he is tolerated but never fully accepted by them. Ever an outsider, occupying a tenuous position at the bureau as a non-gun-carrying employee, he takes stock of the seventeen years he has lived "safe in a demilitarized zone between dick and PR man" (285); and he decides that he has hung on as a stranger among homicide detectives for so long because he is not really so different from them. He admires their sturdy virtues, their loyalty to country and fidelity to home, their contentment with simple pleasures, such as bowling, beer parties, the late show, a fag joke, and sex in one position. Like them, he gets goosebumps when he sees the flag, and he wishes only to be laid to rest with the accolade, "By God, that fella was a good dick" (284). Beset by the domestic crisis of a faithless wife and convinced that he has cop in him, LePeters decides to become a real dick.

Although twice the age of the other fledgling dicks, LePeters' single-minded deliberation triumphs over their "young coltlike muscles" (290) in the one-month training program. On the shooting range his split-second slower firing is backed by judgment, he never guns down pop-ups that prove to be "a poor innocent guy taking a leak in the bushes" but slaughters "only kill-crazy pop-ups who were unmistakably bent on homicide" (290). In crime detection, he quickly develops a skill in analyzing a corpse for clues. He also effortlessly masters the other tricks of his trade: taking notes in a loose-leaf scrapbook rather than a glued notebook, which might contain embarrassing information if introduced into court as evidence; wearing an oversized, stiff-leathered, frontier-type holster from which the gun slides easily; and slipping his free hand casually in his side pocket to provide a steady anchor when firing a revolver. By the time of graduation, he has developed "a clenched and measured new style, hesitating before he spoke, looking at the world with dead eyes—the ideal point of view for a new dick" (290). With his transformation into a full-fledged detective, however, LePeters rejects not only this new self but his previous seventeen years service by resigning from the force. "I'm interested in homicide all right," he tells his startled chief, but "the truth is, I'll never be a dick. I just wanted to see if I could become one" (297).

II *Conformity and the Friedman Hero*

LePeters' aim for seventeen years has been conformity to the rules of a white Anglo-Saxon, Midwestern ethos. He changed his name to fit the stereotype of this group. And his efforts to be a good cop reflect a similar desire to be accepted by the homicide bureau—a certified member of a special group—and a model citizen. Behind the concept of law and order that motivates Le-Peters and the other policemen stands the principle of social conformity. LePeters is more a conformist hero than a non hero or an antihero, for Friedman is drawn to the subject of a big-city police department as much for its conformist revelations as for its social relevance. His depictions of Stern the suburbanite and of Joseph the sophisticate are likewise of aspirants to accepted social behavior, a stance that is almost a convention in the fiction of the 1960's.

In Joseph Heller's portrait of Colonel Cathcart in *Catch-22*, he defines the angst of the small, aspiring, flattened, big, weak *Massenmensch*, or mass man, of our century. Although the nemesis of Yossarian, Colonel Cathcart ironically shares with Yossarian the anxiety that afflicts man faced with his own helplessness and with his insignificance in twentieth-century mass society. An eager student of the rules and taboos of the military, yet Cathcart is perpetually beset with uncertainty. He is "a slick, successful, slipshod, unhappy man of thirty-six who lumbered when he walked and wanted to be a general. . . . He was complacent and insecure, daring in the administrative stratagems he employed to bring himself to the attention of his superiors and craven in his concern that his schemes might all backfire."

For Cathcart not to know at any given moment the moods of his superiors and the situation at General Headquarters is the nightmare of his life: he "was on the alert constantly for every signal, shrewdly sensitive to relationships and situations that did not exist. He was someone in the know who was always striving pathetically to find out what was going on. He was a blustering, intrepid bully who brooded inconsolably over the terrible ineradicable impressions he knew he kept making on people of prominence who were scarcely aware that he was even alive." Colonel Cathcart lives "by his wits in an unstable, arithmetical world of black eyes and feathers in his cap, of overwhelming imaginary triumphs and catastrophic imaginary defeats" (Chap. 19).

Cathcart is not a Byronic superhero, a Promethean Faust, a Vautrin, or a Camusian rebel—his is only the day-to-day fret of the social conformist as distinguished from the cosmic yawp of the Existential rebel. That a Colonel Cathcart is afflicted with angst is understandable, for his ambition to embody his society's ideals is continually frustrated by his failure to understand its rules. He constantly seeks integration with what forever eludes him. The first modern protagonists to exhibit these symptoms of complacency and insecurity were the passive heroes of Sir Walter Scott's Waverley novels. Scott's Edward Waverley, Frank Osbaldistone, Harry Bertram, and Nigel Olifaunt—to name several— are paradigms of "rehearsed responses" to society's construct of values, to law and order, to prudence and restraint. The Waverley hero is, however, the opposite of the Romantic hero; for he forever seeks accommodation with, rather than revolt against, the bureaucratic, the official, and the academic. A forerunner of the twentieth-century functionary, Scott's hero is bent on submission of his thoughts to the emergent utilitarian culture of Georgian England.

The Scott hero, according to Alexander Welsh's perceptive analysis,[2] strives to identify himself with a code of behavior derived not from reality but from the eighteenth-century legal abstraction of property rights. He could still count, however, on a decaying class system firmly based on the actuality of the landed aristocracy. His counterpart in the twentieth century also finds law and order, as well as stability and prudence, desirable; but in today's supermarket culture, he is less certain of what constitutes law and order since the stock beliefs of a corporational society are even more beset by the winds of fashion and by the chimeras of abstraction than were agrarian societies in the past. Group values— manners and economic, political, social ideals—rarely originate or evolve naturally. They derive from arbitrary assertions of the social will that must be learned—and since few guidelines are available or helpful in this continual confrontation, trial and error prevail. Hence, to know what society wishes is an uncertain business; and to sublimate desires to its goal is a frustrating experience, particularly when "getting on" is the chief principle.

Samuel Coleridge in miscellaneous critical remarks about Scott characterized the world of the Waverley novel as one "of *anxiety* from the crown to the hovel, from the cradle to the coffin." "All is an anxious straining to maintain life, or *appearances*," he adds, "to *rise* as the only condition of not falling." [3] This brilliant ascription of what ails the society of the Waverley novels also defines the malaise of Colonel Cathcart's world of the 1940's in which W. H. Auden regarded anxiety as the spirit of the age. The anxious figure of Colonel Cathcart finds his latter-day social role much more difficult to assume than did the Waverley hero, for the world since Scott's day has accelerated its drift toward fragmentation of experience, isolation of the individual, irrelevancy of the future, and the sense of personal inadequacy.

Scott's fictional world of landowning squires presents an appearance of stability and cohesion; but the reality is something else: Scott's age was in transition from an agrarian to an urban society. The traditional hierarchy of values, orderly and unchanging, was crumbling before cultural innovations and accelerating social mobility, terrestrial equivalents to the new world-picture of an organic, ever-expanding universe. Epistemologically, man found himself separated from both the phenomenal and noumenal worlds he inhabited, and only his erring sensibility was a link between him and the outside. The sense of security of the Wordsworth of 1797 to 1807 derived from his belief in man's capacity to bridge the gap between perceiving mind and object perceived and hence in the meaningful relation of man to his environment. But beneath even his calm assertion of order lurked a haunting fear of the old chaos, of flux, and the abdication of authority, which slowly eroded his faith in the transcendental self. This instability Scott defines culturally and historically in terms of the Romantic lawlessness of the Highlands and of the hopeless cause of the Jacobites; but, whatever the name he gives it, the involvement of his passive hero in its disturbing milieu reflects the crisis of consciousness of his time—and of ours.

Since the time of the Waverley hero, society has become increasingly diffuse and contradictory. What was originally a crisis in political economy, complicated by epistemological symptoms, has deepened into a full-blown metaphysical malaise; for in this century society has become a version of the void. This disorientation of man poses new problems for the passive hero, who seeks to realize the authenticity of his self through his identification with its commonplaces. To offset the drift toward entropy, toward chaos, "the black and vasty zephyrs of the Pit," as Ebenezer Cooke more than once characterizes the philosophical vacuum that stares him in the face (*The Sot-Weed Factor*, Chap. 13), today's common man looks to the newest electronic devices for ways of holding together the disintegrating center of experience in some semblance of order. In place of the ordering logic of cause and effect, he substitutes the organizing ratio of average and mean. But, in his eagerness to be average, he submits to a code of behavior more determinedly abstract than that of the Waverley hero; for how else could we account for the nightmarish nature of Colonel Cathcart's world or for the unreality of Eliot Rosewater's sojourn with the ordinary folk living on the ancestral preserve of Rosewater County, Indiana, in Kurt Vonnegut's *God Bless You, Mr. Rosewater.*

Post-World-War-II America has become the product of statisticians' graphs. This computer society is vividly dramatized in the animate-inanimate ambiguities of Thomas Pynchon's V. "Me and SHOCK are what you and everybody will be someday," the robot SHROUD ("Synthetic human, radiation output determined") gibes at Benny Profane (Chap. 19). SHROUD, "five feet nine inches tall—the fiftieth percentile of Air Force standards," is made of a skeleton that had once belonged to a living human; it is covered wtih clear cellulose acetate butyrate; and its lungs, sex organs, kidneys, thyroid, liver, spleen, and other internal organs are designed to measure the amount of radiation which the human body can safely absorb. From Gallup poll estimates to insurance actuary tables, as Pynchon notes, all aspects of life are being geared to a mythical average without flesh and bone—an average that represents no actual person. To serve society's utilitarian end of the collective good, the passive hero has submitted his consciousness of self to a true abstraction.[4] The "century's man," like Herbert Stencil in Pynchon's V., has altered himself, therefore, into "something which does not exist in nature" (Chap. 8). The Waverly hero as a symbol of his society's ideal of the sacred inviolability of property could not act aggressively because of the necessary submission of his will to the principle of law which protects property. The 1960's fictional protagonist as an embodiment of this century's worship of the average cannot relate to any individual because of the reduction of his being to a contrived ratio which renders the extremes of personality non-existent—therefore, the angst of his situation. Prototypical is the Soldier-in-White in Heller's *Catch-22*, who the other patients of the hospital think does not exist beneath his all-enveloping bandages.

Indeed, the world of Heller's *Catch-22*, which exhibits the *ne plus ultra* of man as ratio, is epitomized in Colonel Cathcart's all-purpose form letters of condolence to a dead airman's family. In life, the flier had existed for the military bureaucracy as an entry on a roster list; in death, he becomes an undiscriminated allusion as father-son-husband-nephew-brother. Similar formalities dictate that a dead man's personal effects linger on a bed in Yossarian's tent because their owner was killed before he could report as a replacement. If he was never added to the squadron roster, he cannot now be removed from it. Doc Daneeka suffers a like fate: since his name is on the flight manifesto of a plane that crashed, he is officially described as dead although he continues to walk about the camp as an embarrassing *corpus delicti* of bureaucratic logic.

Like Colonel Cathcart and Scott's passive heroes, Friedman's protagonists are disturbing instances of the solipsism that results when man is thus transformed into a mean. Stern worries about being accepted by a society to whose standard of values he gives whole-hearted assent. He moves his family into the suburbs and frets when his Gentile neighbors reject him. He wants to belong, to keep his lawn groomed and his garden blooming, to support the volunteer fire department by attending its annual ball—but he is unfamiliar with neighborhood protocol. He makes mistakes, lets his garden die, alienates the firemen. When prudence born of fright exhausts him, his stomach blossoms with an ulcer. Even at the Grove Rest Home, where he goes to cure his ulcer, he feels like an interloper, expecting "an entourage of Grove's descendants to run out with clenched fists and veto him" (115). Friedman could not more forcefully indicate that Stern lives in a fantasy world peopled by figments of the social mind.

Stern rarely communicates with another individual, for every-

one presents to him the indistinguishable visage of the stranger.
He even fails to engage in conversation two commuters regalent
with camaraderie, and he is equally unable to talk to his mother
or his father. He meets his wife only on the most unsatisfactory
of sexual levels. Acquaintances, who are similarly products of the
mean, might as well not exist for him. When he attempts in his
self-doubt and imaginary fears to reach out to a friend for personal contact, he is told to abstract himself—advice that could
hardly be less suitable for a person already suffering from the
dissociation of the average!

Joseph is likewise frustrated in his effort to adjust to the national norm—to the customs of a fraternity, the nuances of the
classroom, the etiquette of a restaurant, the affectations of girls,
the code of the corner dance hall. He is desperate to accommodate his conduct to the standards of an affluent society. Nervous
because he and his mother are the only Jews at a party given by
Irish Catholics, he gauchely starts a fight and is led away in
shame by his mother. He writhes under the scorn he presumes
everyone feels for him when, by mid-summer, he has not yet been
accepted by a college.

Similarly, LePeters is emotionally drained by living the pseudo-
identity of an unofficial detective. With sickening dependence,
he has followed his boss Bruno Glober through a nameless number of police departments, relying on Glober "as a buffer zone
between [him] and the frightening, unknown world of higher-
ups." Constantly frightened by the tough homicide detectives,
LePeters is "the heartiest laugher in the bureau" (57) when a
joke is told or a gag pulled; and he is always gratified to see
others in the showers, gunless and pot-bellied, for a moment
seemingly harmless civilians. When out of uniform, the detectives
affect "wide, loose-fitting slacks with a great floating sag at the
crotch" (52)—and LePeters has his pants designed in that fashion,
"to be one of the boys" (52).

Stern, Joseph, and LePeters are all reduced to pseudo-exis-
tences. By such means Friedman dramatizes the identity crisis
afflicting man in the ecumenical anonymity of contemporary
American culture. Dependent on appearance for a sense of their
authenticity, theirs is the excruciating pain of not feeling themselves to be fully defined individuals. In this world which sets
great store on conformity, clothes acquire transcendent value.

Dress is also a desperate concern of the Waverly hero; it determines the treatment accorded to others and received in return. Clothes allow one to distinguish the collective stance from Romantic gestures of disruptive lawlessness. God-fearing, upright Jeannie Dean, in *The Heart of the Midlothian,* is treated with suspicion as disreputable and hence as a threat to order when Maud Wildfire drags her dusty and bedraggled into church. Frank Osbaldistone, in *Rob Roy,* nervously frets about his appearance when he arrives travel-worn at the country house of his uncle; and he reacts with moral bewilderment to Diane Vernon's disheveled, loose-flowing dress at their first meeting. Scott carefully identifies his madmen by their outlandish garb.

It is not insignificant then nor wholly accidental that Friedman in a contemporary treatment of mass manners has his characters depend heavily on this traditional social sign. Thus, LePeters takes comfort in the fraternity of police uniform and of baggy civilian trousers. But dress can also make one an outsider, as LePeters nervously notes when he tours the New York City "hip" scene one night and finds himself among sleek, continentally styled men and women. Worse, dress can falsify, as in the case of LePeters each time he dons his police uniform and pins on his badge; and this possibility plagues Stern's desire to be part of a group. The uniformity of dress in today's mass society prevents him from knowing how to act, thereby complicating his uncertain *rapprochement* to people. In the Air Force, everyone wears the same uniform, making fliers and nonfliers, Jews and Gentiles, look-alikes. On the commuter train, everyone is garbed in the same indistinguishable businessman's gray. At the Grove Rest Home, the ubiquitous bathrobe and slippers effectively camouflage personal differences.

Both Stern and LePeters learn the hard way that the uniformity of contemporary society is a false unity, a heterogeneity masquerading as homogeneity. Beneath the sameness of masks riots a profound diversity, posing for the eager conformist the bated breath and uncertainty of a misstep. No wonder then that Stern is upset because "there was no way to tell by looking" that his employer Belavista had three million dollars: "He might have been a man with $300,000 or even $27,500, and Stern felt if you had millions, there ought to be a way for people to tell this at a glance. A badge you got to wear or a special millionaire's necktie" (89). And it is no wonder that LePeters finds the homicide detectives disconcertingly heterogeneous: Teener, despite his whittled-down person, occasionally flares into the icy gunman he once had been; Medici, under his bland detective facade, is still the touchy black; and Gibney, despite his cynicism as an "ace vice-squadder" (194), cries like a baby when a fellow officer turns renegade and becomes a killer.

The homogenization of dress in modern society has aggravated twentieth-century man's loss of a sense of personal authenticity. Ironically, the goal sought—conformity as the acme of normality —has rendered the individual more vulnerable and isolated than ever before. Disturbed by this unexpected fact, ordinary man recoils paradoxically from the sober prudence of society in favor of the coherence of self: he becomes the "hippy" making his scene all alone. Sebastian Dangerfield in Donleavy's *The Ginger Man* is the conformist hero turned inside out, a conformist *manqué*, in raging protest against the uniformity of the bourgeois ideal. His is a rascally parody of the ultra-respectable citizen with excellent credit rating.[5] Samson Sillitoe in Elliott Baker's *A Fine Madness* is similarly parodic of the Romantic poet, for he is goaded into resistance to the conformist regimen of the utilitarian world.

These characters are the end product of the Romantic assertion of self in a liberal tradition, which posits as its standard the greatest good for the greatest number. Both are mass men, who choose isolation because they recognize it as the inadvertent consequence of mass accommodation. But, as Sebastian is constantly learning to his discomfort, man cannot dissociate himself entirely from the world. Unfortunately now, however, when a Stern or a Sebastian Dangerfield seeks to relate to another, he speaks out of the fixed solipsism of his own jerry-built scene. He is an imprisoned "I," an integer absorbed by the penchant for the average, lacking in the skill or will to contact a "Thou." Rather than addressing an individual in a meaningful meld of sensibilities, he talks past the person. The irrelevancy of such converse confirms his dread of dislocation and increases his sense of anxiety. The obliquity of dissonance rather than the union of confrontation prevails.

Much of the laughter of disquiet in Friedman's writing derives from this dramatic situation in which people speak to but fail to reach one another. Home from the doctor's, where an examination has disclosed an ulcer, Stern finds his mother and father there but his wife out. "Isn't your wife home when you have an ulcer?" his mother asks incongruously, as if ulcers come and go with the regularity of the evening meal or with the frequency of headaches. "She doesn't know about it yet," Stern replies. Automatically, as if the exchange between Stern and his mother had not just occurred, his father chimes in, "She ought to be home if you're not feeling well" (108). Such scenes occur frequently in the pages of Friedman's stories, for they are the ordinary currency of his people's lives. Worried about getting into college, Joseph asks his mother for advice; and she answers, "The money will be there." "I don't mean that. I don't know which ones to send off to," he replies. "Don't worry about the money," she continues. "We'll get it somehow. It'll be there" (10). The multiplication of Joseph's uncertainty after his talk with his mother is understandable, for her assurance has increased rather than lessened his distress. Words, a bridge linking one person to another, have served only to widen the breach between Joseph's adolescent problem and her adult misunderstanding of it. Friedman dramatizes the generation gap here; even more profoundly, he demonstrates how uniformity, the ideal of the social conformist, is self-defeating because it limits him to the caprice of his own locked-in sensibility. Such communal isolation feeds the Friedman hero's sense of personal isolation.

III *In Search of a New Life Style*

We need emphasize, despite the remarks of the previous section, that Friedman's protagonists are ambivalent in their urge to conformity; for Stern both wishes to deny his Jewishness and to continue to be a Jew; Joseph longs for release from maternal domination and for continuation of its security; and LePeters pretends that he is a steely-eyed detective, a full-fledged member of the blue-coated fraternity, while deploring its life of daily violence and blood-letting. All three men are psychologically divided, as is underscored by the irony of Stern's name and by the scar that runs the length of LePeters' face, splitting it from forehead to chin and giving his pleasant features "a curiously divided look" (4).

Unlike Stern and Joseph, however, who continue on the razor's edge, LePeters moves off the dead center of personal incompleteness and social ostracism. He acts to alter his life style by taking the leap into a new identity. He rejects the work ethic and assumes a relaxed sexual attitude. If the narrative of each Friedman novel is directed toward initiation of its protagonist into a sense of personal authenticity, with Stern and Joseph unable within the context of the narrative to achieve full metamorphosis of their beings, then LePeters can be said to have succeeded in realizing on the psychosexual level a new social role.

Besides the problems LePeters faces as a "quasi-dick" (16) in a homicide bureau, he is coping with a series of domestic (and personal) crises. He purchases a house, which he discovers too late is "lipped over by a few feet or so into another district" (59), a poverty area, necessitating that his ten-year-old daughter attend an all-black school. Egged on by his wife Claire, he investigates the quality of the school, its teachers and its educational program, with the intention of requesting a transfer of his daughter into the town's predominantly white school. But he timidly postpones any action for over a year, to the disgust of his wife; and he rationalizes to himself that his daughter's teachers are first-rate and that her black friends are giving her a rounded education in the ways of all kinds of people.

Ironically, given the vulgar puns on his name and on his occupation, LePeters and his wife have always lived together at best in "sexual truce," she "making her lean whiplike Minnesota body available to him for one or two positions at the most, but still electing to keep her lips private" (41). The rest of the time she freezes him by dangling precariously on her side of the bed, her back to him. Only minimally imaginative or adventurous sexually, LePeters is occasionally tempted by other women, especially by Cissy Glober, his boss's free-wheeling, nubile daughter; but he remains generally faithful as tension builds in him from his anxieties at the homicide bureau, his apprehensions about his daughter's ghetto friends, and his frustrations caused by his wife's rejections. Finally, one night, after coming home to find his daughter "lynched" (that is, trussed and hanging from a tree, but alive and kicking) by her black playmate Samantha and after being repulsed in his desire to make love to his wife, he decides "to get

away and think things over before it all goes down the drain"
(141).

Thus begins for him months of emotional disorder and sexual
irregularity. When he goes to a Caribbean island for a "singles"
holiday, he meets frank-speaking, generous-minded Ellen Rosenberg, who specializes in "shoring up the confidence of . . . emotionally shell-torn" (175) men. After spending a night with her,
he takes flight, rushing back conscience-stricken to his wife. For
a while his new self-confidence rallies his wife's sexual interest;
but typically he falls "a bit shy" of bringing her to "the finish
line" (190). At a Homicide and Aggravated Battery Gala, Claire
LePeters meets ex-Detective Chico, now in movie making, with
whom she begins an affair. In retaliation, LePeters resumes his
affair with Ellen Rosenberg, but his extramarital conquest proves
to be only partial consolation for his anguish of mind over his
wife's continuing infidelity. One night, when he discovers that
Ellen Rosenberg is also unfaithful to him, he suddenly feels re-
leased from years of "unhappy, tightly manacled dependency"
on women—as a son on his mother, then as a husband on his
wife, and most recently as a lover, the "suffocating reliance on
Ellen" (268).

A period of LePeters' life begins in which he rushes through
"a series of affairlets, brief, tense, sexual interviews which he
would cut off suddenly so he could dash off to conduct another"
(272); he is in frenzied pursuit of finding "out a few things
about women" (268). Returning home late one night he finds
that his wife has gone with Detective Chico to help shoot a picture. Noting that she has not taken all her dresses, he realizes that
she will return. He is amazed, and relieved, at his powers of
adjustment to the situation and at his ability to survive it emotionally. While in this mood to endure, he decides to attend the
police academy; but he graduates as a detective only to reject a
career, since this success does not resolve his domestic crisis. In
the dénouement, he terminates his affairs before assuming a new
identity by shooting two toes off the foot of his wife's lover, by
rejecting his wife's overtures of reconciliation, by taking his ten-
year-old daughter from school, and by departing on an un-
designated trip with her to start a new life.

Another personal problem that LePeters resolves has to do with
the memory of his father, who his mother has always claimed

had been disgracefully exploited by Frickman Furs where he had worked for forty-five years. A measure of LePeters' new maturity is his recognition when he calls on the Frickmans, gun in his pocket and murder in his heart, that the family tradition "existed entirely in the head of his mother." Instead of his father's dropping dead from "the supposedly tough grinding hours he had spent on the job," they had been the happiest of his life. "The truth was, instead of being a furnace of hell for him, Frickman Furs had been his father's lifeblood"; the real hell had been "his home and the tough, ever-complaining Flo Sussman" (262–63). "Feeling cleaner and hundreds of pounds lighter than when he had arrived," LePeters leaves the Frickmans with "a central lie of his existence . . . eradicated" (264).

LePeters' domestic difficulties prove to be the catalyst which leads him to rebel against those weekend get-togethers "with other crime-busting families" in "combination volleyball games and charcoal cookouts," where he had been "treading water, splashing around in the temporary" (7), and to seek a new life style that stretches his abilities—and that incidentally ignores society's conventions. His stint in the police academy confirms for him his illimitable capacity for existence: he knows it was "Through fierce application and a flexing of those muscles available to him, that he had managed to breeze right through the course." Suddenly a free soul, he "wondered what other unthinkably difficult skills he might be able to master. Could he build a cabinet? Pilot a salvage ship through the China seas? Why others, and not LePeters? Though half of his life had gone by the boards, he saw now that it was an inferior half and that the remaining section might very well turn out to be terrific" (297). He could spend his days comfortably now in "carefree morning sleep" without feeling guilty about not carrying on "the family's workbound tradition" (302). He could take the squad car out to the highway and watch "the bumper to bumper parade of infuriated fellows on their way to the city, LePeters himself comfortably sailing along in the opposite lane." It was as if he were recovered at last from a disease after long years of travail "a free fellow" (302).

LePeters' escape from fixed modes of thought and action is achieved not without pain and trauma. He must die to his old self if he would metamorphose into the LePeters who sallies forth toward an unknown destination with his daughter, joyously embracing a "new freedom" (301).

At first, his rebellion against the rigidity and conformism of the police world is ambiguous. He views with horror the placard saying "Welcome, Future Policewoman," which his daughter dutifully hangs above her bed, as prescribed in a letter by Chief Guster: "To be posted in the room of every progeny of a police officer and not to be taken down under any circumstances unless a written explanation form is filed with this department." Sufficiently subservient at the time to be unable to throw the offensive placard away, his rebellion extends to yanking it off the wall and shoving it "away off to the side behind her toybox, technically in her room but where she would rarely if ever glance at the damned thing" (102–3).

It is the pull of society in respect to his family which eventually prompts LePeters whole-heartedly to accept his position as an uprooted transient American, "a veteran of short stays in dozens of pinched-off little villages" (46). In the matter of his daughter's school he resists accommodation with the establishment, pulling vehemently against the norm for reasons not always explicable to him. Hence, although he hates as much as does his wife having his daughter in an all-black school, "Yet he could not bring himself to yank her out. It was not just a question of being paralyzed by indecision. . . . It was something more, buried in the rubble of his mind, that he hadn't bent down to pick around for" (81).

In the chronicle of this breakthrough into the limitless possibilities of the heterogeneous, Friedman gives us a parable for our times, thereby crystallizing for us a way of life central to increasing numbers of Americans. As the four-day week is almost upon us, a leisure world hitherto undreamt of by man looms ahead; but whether it will be a boon or a new purgatory is still uncertain. The only certainty is that our lives will be different, that individuality will have scope for realization, indeed will probably require greater expression than was possible under the scarcity economies of the past. The pluralism of experiments in communal living, with its demands on human imagination and its multiplication of chances for failure, has already become a part of the landscape of America. Without making an explicit case for this, or some other, life style of the future, Friedman has presented LePeters' alteration of goals as yet another instance historically of the rites of passage by means of which man wins through to new stages of being. In *The Dick*, as contrasted to *Stern* and *A Mother's Kisses*, Friedman opts for positive action, for a loud *yea* to the unknown possibilities in human nature.

IV *Fixations and Mannerisms*

If the affirmative note struck at the end of *The Dick* represents an effort by Friedman to extend his consciousness of American society in the last quarter of the twentieth century, his mechanics of fictional narration and habits of stylistic expression have hardened through familiarity into mannerism. After three novels, two plays and over fifty short stories, it has become clear that certain fixations, frankly acknowledged in his uncamouflaged repetition of them in narrative after narrative, release Friedman's imagination. It is not easy to assign causes to these fixations, but they may derive from deep-seated anxieties in Friedman's psyche, or they may just as likely reflect current tensions in American society. Their recurrence does not necessarily indicate a weakening of conceptual control when—as in *Stern* and *A Mother's Kisses*—they are intensely felt by the author. But in *The Dick* these materials are too often seized upon for an unearned resolution of plot. LePeters' decision to take a "luxury vacation" (145) without his wife is not so well motivated as Stern's flight to a rest home. In this third novel, the gimmicks of mild nervous breakdown, recuperative trip, and sexual adventure have degenerated into formula. The same can be said for the recurrence of the gadget-geared cripple, the aggressive harridan of a mother, the slavey father, the sexually errant wife, the frantic cuckolded husband, the bare-brained but rich relative, and the dumb but loyal black helper. Of interest in this regard is how *The Dick* loses narrative direction when Friedman begins to introduce these motifs midway in the novel. Instead of aiding in his exploration of the themes of law and order and of social conformity, they bind his imagination to the riskless and manipulative quotient.

Nor does Friedman's prose style maintain the capacity, as in the earlier novels, to suggest meaning beyond the literal content of the statement. There are instances of authentic social observation: LePeters' perception, for example, of the workaday world as a salvation for his father (262–63); his revulsion at the "atmosphere of death" (239) that permeates the life of the detectives; and his genuine wonderment at his daughter's study projects on "Paraguay, Past and Present," Italian castles, and furniture of the Georgian and Federal periods—a program which seems to him "scattered, unplanned, as though a special colored division at the board of education had decided not to give them any shit, as long as they stayed quiet and didn't go around knifing each other" (125–26). Too often, however, Friedman is satisfied with the cheaply won laugh that depends on a tag line, like the Negro school principal's dental-flawed speech, which issues "dits" and "dats" between words, as if her thoughts were coded in Morse; or an elaborate put-on for the sake of a two-word joke, like the to-do about LePeters' hernia, which allows Friedman to characterize LePeters as "broken-balled" (115), a not very funny allusion to his sexual difficulties with his wife; or on the reversal of a cliché, as when wealthy, cultured black parents remove their daughter from a ghetto school because eighteen children of a slatternly, poor-white Carolinian family also attend it (281).

Friedman has relied heavily, in the past, on his language to develop character and to convey theme, as well as to build mood and atmosphere; and *The Dick* is no exception. Where we detect a deterioration of tension in this novel, we are responding probably as much as anything to his elimination of the stylistic disjunction between rhetoric and situation which works so well in *Stern* and in *A Mother's Kisses*. In *The Dick*, Friedman has foregone the mood and setting of the sentimental 1940's for the pornographic, blasé 1970's; and his rhetoric partakes of the same ethos. Consequently, it risks sounding more mundane and hackneyed than in *Stern;* but his ear, for the most part, still captures the peculiarities of speech and rhythms of thought of the ordinary and the commonplace. Like the Rumanian-French dramatist Eugene Ionesco, Friedman has a talent for giving esthetic relevance to the inanities of speech and dramatic point to the most puerile of situations; and he habitually conceives his stories in the form of short, dramatic episodes. It is not surprising then that, after mastering the skills of fiction, he should turn to writing plays. It is more surprising that he waited so long before making the attempt.

CHAPTER *6*

Plays and Other Writings

I Scuba Duba

FRIEDMAN'S first play, *Scuba Duba,* a "Tense Comedy," opened at the New Theater on October 10, 1967; directed by Jacques Levy, it starred Jerry Orbach, the musical comedy star, as Harold Wonder and Brenda Smiley as the zany, bikini-clad girl next door. The play was acclaimed next morning by *New York Times* drama critic Clive Barnes as "the most polished and certainly the most hilarious American comedy since Arthur Kopit's 'Oh Dad, Poor Dad.' . . . [altogether] a most distinguished debut for Mr. Friedman, and an Off Broadway hit that most Broadway should see." [1] Within a day or two the advance sale of tickets had run through six months into April of the following year; and the play was settling down for a two-year run in its comfortable quarters just off Broadway.

No one was more surprised than Friedman to find that he had a "hit" on his hands. Yet his "instant" success in the theater does not quite fit the young-man-up-from-the-provinces image; for since boyhood, he has enjoyed peripheral links with Shubert Alley. His mother worked part-time in Broadway box offices off and on for years; his father had played a piano in the pit for silent films; and his father's sister had functioned as assistant treasurer at the Broadhurst. Friedman still has not forgotten the thrill of seeing Judy Canova and Buddy Ebsen in *Yokel Boy* and Abbott and Costello in *Streets of Paris.* "Whenever there was a show that bombed," he recalls, "we'd get free tickets to it from my aunt. I remember seeing 'The Star Crossed Story' with Eva Le Gallienne, and I guess that was my first lesson in play-writing. I realized even then that the entire play was over when the curtain came up because the characters just stood around having great thoughts about it." [2] The drama critic incipient in this remark was given the chance to emerge when, at the University of Missouri, he made a stab at drama reviewing for the university daily; but after a dozen reviews his nasty remarks about a Stephens College production of Thornton Wilder's *Our Town* created such an uproar that he vacated his critic's armchair.

Friedman's adventures on the other side of the footlights, while not extensive, have been of longer duration than the overnight acclaim of *Scuba Duba* might suggest. Several years prior to the comedy, his instinctive feel for the theater had already caught the eye of men in the entertainment world. The ultimate end of Friedman's fictional impatience with narrative description and with elaborate buildup of character is dramatic form of some sort. His prose also supports this tendency with its nervous movement of speech and its continual lapse into extended dialogues. And in one of his stories, "Car Lover" (*Esquire,* June, 1968), he has reduced the entire scene and situation to a dialogue between a car salesman and a prospective buyer. Predictably, this narrative was picked up by Stage 73 and integrated into a larger program of adaptations for the theater. Friedman did not like the way it was being handled, however, and withdrew the work during previews. The program, as it then existed, was subsequently dropped; but part of it showed up as *Adaptation-Next* in an off-Broadway show in 1969.

At least two other of his stories have been tapped as being inherently dramatic. "23 Pat O'Brien Movies," whose supple dialogue is one of the best things that Friedman has written, was used as an exercise by the students of Frank Corsaro's acting class; and Corsaro also tried to get Actor's Studio to do it as part of a two-day evening Off Broadway. After he and Cheryl Crawford had fooled with the idea and then finally dropped it, the American Place Theater found out about the script and produced it under Gaby Lieber's direction for their subscription group. Along with another play and some short films on the bill, it ran for the allotted three weeks. At Friedman's request, no critics were sent to review it. "Show Biz Connections" was tried out as one of the skits for the musical *The Apple Tree,* which Mike Nichols directed and which ran for a year and a half at the Shubert Theater in 1966–67; but it was dropped after rehearsals began. There has also been an attempt at a musical version of *A Mother's Kisses,* with music and lyrics by Richard Adler, and libretto by Friedman. It reached the out-of-town, pre-Broadway stage, opening in New Haven and closing at the Morris Mechanic Theater, Baltimore, during the first weeks of October, 1968.

Friedman made his first calculated move toward the theater in the summer of 1966 when he quit Magazine Management to write a screen adaptation of Jock Carroll's novel *The Shy Photographer* for the movie producer Alan Pakula. Although a first draft was completed by November, 1966, the script has never been produced; and it is unlikely that it ever will. Friedman candidly admits that he undertook the screen-writing assignment because "there was absolutely nothing in the book I could use." [3] Its satire is directed primarily at what is described as the phony, hard-drinking, girl-chasing, routine of journalism and at the arty pretensions of magazine photography, little of which would have appealed to Friedman's social consciousness. The best things about the scenario are his own incidental high-spirited jabs at American sacred cows: the annual Beauty Queen industry, the status symbols of American business, the cradle-to-grave paternalism of government, the dishonesty and disloyalty of employees, the man-of-the-year and the story-of-the-year ballyhoo of the journalistic world. In effect, Friedman tried to write a new story; but the concentration of the irony of the novel on the theme of the artist's inhuman obligation to the demands of his art proved to be intractable; he could not divert the narrative into the special areas of human relationship that kindle his imagination. Furthermore, the deadpan tone, inane characters, and extravagant situations offered his sensibility no psychosexual ambience of the kind to which he responds. Ultimately, Friedman has written a script foreign to his talents; the staccato scenes are closer to the cool, distanced delirium of Terry Southern's *Candy* and *The Magic Christian* than to the tense, involved mania of *Stern* and *A Mother's Kisses*.

After the painful lesson of *The Shy Photographer*, Friedman decided in 1968 not to do "The Lennie Bruce Story," which Marvin Worth at Columbia Pictures had asked him to work on. He contracted to read through the transcripts and published material about Bruce, as a prelude to making up his mind about accepting the assignment. Modestly, he offers as his reason for not taking it his conviction that, since he could not figure out what Lennie would say or do in any given situation, the picture would have wound up being about himself—and he did not think that was fair.

In 1969, he agreed, however, to work on the film *The Owl and the Pussycat*. And since then he has moved toward an unformalized association with the movie industry. His story "Change of Plan" has been filmed by Palomar Productions with Neil Simon doing the screenplay and Elaine May directing it. Cybill Shepherd, Eddie Albert, and Jeannie Berlin (Elaine May's daughter) appear in the movie which showed with much ballyhoo early in 1973. Friedman has also worked on the film script of *The Dick* for Warner Brothers; but there are no immediate plans for production.

The earliest version of *Scuba Duba* antedates by a full year Friedman's courageous divorce from the financial security of Magazine Management and his diffident liaison with the movie industry. The history of the play's metamorphosis from short story to tense comedy illustrates the characteristic nexus of narrative and dramatic in the deep well of Friedman's imagination. He scribbled a draft of the story in an all-night stint during a two-month summer vacation in 1965 in a rented "six-bedroom candy castle" villa on the Riviera in Cap d'Antibes.[4] In subsequent rewrites, Friedman developed the narrative into its present dramatic form.

Friedman insists that this switch in genre was forced upon him by his subject matter: "too terrible for a book, too raw, and, since it took place all in one evening, as just right for a play." [5] *Scuba Duba* bares the bone-marrow depth of the American obsession with the black man. The situation is so familiar in the folklore of the white-black confrontation in America as to be almost a cliché. While on vacation in a rented chateau in the south of France, the white mother of two children deserts her husband, a writer of billboard copy, for a Brooks Brothers, button-down-collar Negro who writes poetry of an academic sort (he is proud of an acceptance by *Partisan Review*). For a while Harold Wonder, the betrayed husband, mistakenly believes that his wife is running off with a rascally sexed-up black scuba diver, whom he had befriended out of a self-concious white latitudinarianism. Discovery of the real object of his wife's affections, the respectable, educated Reddington, does not assuage his anguish over his wife's liaison with a Negro. In the past, Harold had indulgently overlooked his wife's occasional philanderings; now, he alternately snarls and whimpers, racked by conflict between his liberal Jewish conscience and his white man's outrage. Through a long night of despair, in a strange country, he appeals to family and strangers alike. He exchanges pent-up grudges with his mother by transatlantic phone; he invites for a visit his analyst, who is vacationing in a nearby village; he spills everything to a nubile next-door neighbor; finally, *vis-à-vis* the two Negroes and his wife, who has come for her belongings, he mouths all the fears that are aroused in the white man by the black man. All the alien, irrational myths about the black man's violent nature and sexual prowess that the white liberal ordinarily restricts to the fringes of his consciousness tumble forth in a purgative confrontation of the two races.

Leslie A. Fiedler has written of the nightmarish world of racially tainted America that its "white, largely European settlers . . . have had, from the earliest times, to work out their personal fates and national destiny in the presence of two alien races." Consequently, "Deep in the mind of America there exist side by side a dream and a nightmare . . . of the American frontier of the West (where the second race is the Indian), or of the South (where the second race is the Negro)." [6] Much of the immediate impact of *Scuba Duba* comes from the physical presence of the two races in a head-on clash—a clash that the machinery of society and the isolation of the ghetto ordinarily keep muted and distant—in which each hurls gutter invectives at the other and in which each gives reality to otherwise half-formulated misconceptions. But the real psychological horror, which the play forces upon our consciousness, is one of recognition. With shocked reluctance we are compelled to reassess our deepest responses to alien races, and to admit that our cherished ideal of social ecumenicalism is a thin, liberal veneer pasted over a rough-hewn primordial terror of loss of racial identity.

In this play, Friedman demands that the white liberal face the full implications of his ethics. Why does Harold Wonder invite Foxtrot, the Frogman, into a camaraderie with himself and his wife? As Jean Wonder reminds her husband, their unlikely friendship with Foxtrot was "A Harold Wonder special." "You like him," she sneers; "you can't live without him. I'll tell you what—pick up the phone, make a reservation and the two of you can go flying down to Rio" (76).[7] The deep guilt of the white liberal, Friedman says, prompts Harold to befriend Foxtrot; but, when Harold is asked to make the ultimate offering of his white wife as an earnest of his sincerity, he balks. The invasion of his home by the blacks in the second act becomes a powerful metaphor of the predicament of the white liberal American, faced with the total demand of the black for redress of centuries of neglect. At one point, Harold irritatedly asks his wife to stop her nervous, compulsive dusting of the furniture. "There's something that happens to your shoulders—when you dust," he complains; "and I don't want to get involved in that now" (69). *Involvement* is a key term in the current scene between whites and blacks; and, in the inadvertent disclaimer of Harold, Friedman ironically reminds us of the all-or-nothing promise of the liberal gesture if it is to be meaningful and effective. The naïveté of Harold in racial matters is pinpointed by his last name, Wonder. Even more effectively, his infantile range of feeling for the black, alternately benevolence and hostility, is perfectly underscored by the lethal scythe he carries about absentmindedly like Linus' security blanket.[8]

The Black Humor of the play does not restrict itself, however, to a diagnosis of the white liberal's hangup; for it acridly depicts a wide range of racial and national prejudices: the white conservative outlook, the Black image of self, the French view of the American, and vice versa. As a social realist, Friedman seeks in this play "to get at the tissue of what race is about, what Negro means, and what kind of strong feelings national consciousness generates." [9] Thus, the militancy of the white conservative is portrayed in the character of the American Tourist, who is shown Harold's villa as a prospective tenant. Addressing Foxtrot, the Tourist says," "I've been watching you awhile, Foxtrot, and I just want to say right now that I respect you as a man. You're coming through loud and clear and nasty and I can hear you. Now I'm white and you're one of those black guys, but just one man to another—me standing here, you standing way the hell over there. . . ." In mockingly servile tone, Foxtrot's rejoinder parodies the role of Black Sambo that he interprets the "you're a man, and I'm a man" pitch of the Tourist to mean "I respect you too, man. I'm going to give you something. I'm going to give you a shine." But Foxtrot's tone changes as his words become aggressively threatening: "I'm gonna shine up your ass. Hey, shine 'em up, shine 'em up." And he chases after the frightened Tourist (81).

Similarly, Jean Wonder romanticizes the much-vaunted Negro capacity for "soul." She contrasts her husband's emotional blocks with her Negro lover's easy access to deep feeling. Negroes "say things that are beyond your wildest imaginings," she taunts Harold, whose inhibitions condemn him to one-handed lovemaking. "Do you know they even recite poetry to women" (74). But the sentiments we finally hear from the lips of her black lover are so dated and so prone to treakle that they would bring a blush to the cheeks of Edna St. Vincent Millay. "What matter cakes or wine or tasty bouillabaisse," he recites, "When love lies bruised and clotted on the thin and punished lips of our American black dream . . ." (82). "Wait here and I'll be back," he soothingly assures Jean at one point in their exchange with Harold, "though the hours divide, and the city streets, perplexed, perverse, delay my hurrying footstep . . ." (86). To this inflated rhetoric, Harold justly rejoins with a poem of his own: "Intruders ye be . . . make haste, abandon this place . . ./Or I'll punch that spade in his colored face" (83).

Beneath all the wise cracks, the pleas for integration, and the ideals of racial co-existence, there continue a basic distrust and ignorance. Masks have been worn so long that they are mistaken for reality, and pseudo identities prevail. Friedman touches on this factor of continued misunderstanding when he has Harold reply to an angry retort of Reddington: "The main thing is I can outwrite you, I can outfight you, I can outthink you. . . ." To this outrageous claim of white superiority, Foxtrot leeringly answers, "Yeah, but there's one thing you can't *out* him, babe. That man there *(With a sly sexual gesture)* is a colored man" (83).

Despite its many comic elements, *Scuba Duba* is a sobering play. The Tourist may be full of hilarious prejudices about different nationalities: "It's the Italians you got to watch. The important thing is to keep them away from shiny stuff. Rings, silverware, tinfoil. Drives 'em crazy. . . . Any time you invite an Italian person over, make sure you don't have anything around that makes a jingling sound" (80). The French Landlady may amuse us with her addled fixations about movie stars and about her own sexual allure: she sees every person improbably as a Hollywood celebrity susceptible to her physical charms. The bikini-clad Miss Janus may enchant us with her suggestive posturings and ingénue accounts of erotically pointless stories.

But each also sinisterly contributes to the terrors of Harold's long night of trying to make contact with another human being. The Tourist plays on the exposed nerve ends of Harold's racial prejudice. The Landlady and Miss Janus exacerbate his sexual fears. Haunted by the half-truths of his society and by the ludicrous despair of the cuckold, he is also unnerved by the well-meaning insensitivity of strangers who wander in and out of his house. Seeking desperately to "reach" another person, he communicates all night with landladies and stray tourists, transient next-door neighbors, burglars, and slight acquaintances, a psychiatrist and his sexually intemperate patient. He appeals to his mother in a long-distance call when he is forced to substitute a telephone line for the umbilical cord that his despair cries out for; and he ends by mentioning some of her sexual indiscretions, thereby becoming more estranged than ever.

Richard Gilman, writing in *The New Republic,* has denounced *Scuba Duba* as "an ersatz play, a shopping bag of attitudes and awarenesses plucked from others' shelves, not an act of freedom or a revolutionary move into a dimension that transcends previous categories of taste." [10] Friedman substitutes a "vocabulary of insult and invective" in lieu of his "failure to achieve any kind of dramatic structure." [11] Without wishing to imply that the play breaks free of convention into fresh extensions of dramatic form, we can detect in Gilman's attack a certain imperceptivity when confronting the structure of *Scuba Duba.* A veteran theater critic, Gilman may be excused for not recognizing the methods of the novelist; for although the second act of *Scuba Duba* has a conventional dramatic confrontation, the play as a whole follows novelistic lines of development. Act I consists of a series of random contacts between Harold and others: Miss Janus, the Landlady, the American Tourist, an analyst, and a French burglar. The thematic reverberations of these encounters recur in stark form like a leitmotif in Act II when Harold is confronted with his wife, her lover Reddington, and Foxtrot.

Similarly, the stock characters so reminiscent of the Broadway theater, and the "insult and invective" of human beings so reflective of the Albee sensibility (which Friedman admires), when these are translated to a new battleground, can be seen with a shift in perspective as deriving with equal validity from the *raison d'être* of Black Humor. Granted this ancestry, Friedman's use of stereotypes becomes a daring articulation of the social conformist of Black Humor in the prevailing morphology of the stage.

Still, an element of truth resides in Gilman's strictures, for Friedman's language remains his greatest strength. Its up-to-date idiom and bouncy rhythms, although highly stylized, read so naturally that they are seemingly custom made for the theater. His juxtapositions of words and ideas which deflate, surprise, or shock are inherently dramatic; and they suggest not only personal confrontation but also inner conflict. "Harold, you're on your own. I can't carry you any longer," Dr. Schoenfeld says, preparatory to his final exit. "It's time you got up on your own two feet and faked your way into the adult community" (96). With these words, Friedman introduces a new side not only to Harold's ruthless infantilism but also to mankind's, and Harold's "security" scythe and his aggressive use of "graffiti" synonyms for the word *Negro* support the shock of recognition. Friedman depends heavily in *Scuba Duba* on this capacity for the drama instinctive in his language.

As a man of the theater, however, Friedman recognizes that he can rely too heavily on his talent for words: "I learned with this play to trust the actor with my idea, not hobble him with speeches all the time." "If I write another play," he confessed at the time, "I'll give the actors more leeway. Fewer verbal expressions of emotion. It is enough to indicate that anger is to be shown. An actor can think up ways to reveal this feeling as easily as I can." [12]

With the success of *Scuba Duba*, Friedman glimpsed the possibilities of a career as a dramatist. Whereas he had before soaked up indiscriminately whatever came to his attention as an intelligent playgoer, he now conscientiously began to see most of the experimental shows in New York City. He is fascinated by the possibilities of drama and by its aura of risk and threat. "I like the danger the theater creates," he told an interviewer in San Francisco at the opening of a road-show company of *Scuba Duba*.[13]

II   Steambath

Friedman's next drama, *Steambath*, opened off-Broadway at the Truck and Warehouse Theater on June 30, 1970. The lead role of Tandy was played by Anthony Perkins, who also doubled as director. In general, the play was well received by the critics; and it ran for almost four months. Toward the end of its run, another novelist-turned-playwright, Kurt Vonnegut, Jr., began to enjoy his maiden success with an off-Broadway production of his play *Happy Birthday, Wanda June*. During the strike of Actor's Equity against the off-Broadway theaters from November 17 to December 17, the decision was made to move Vonnegut's play to the small Edison Theater in the Time's Square area, where it continued as a modest attraction of the season. Although the plays are basically dissimilar in their comments on man, they have much in common besides their fortunes at the box office and the novelistic backgrounds of their authors.

For an understanding of Friedman's dramatic instincts, we may profitably compare his play with Vonnegut's. Both plays utilize the time-worn device of a setting in the afterlife, whose prototype in this century is Sutton Vane's play of the 1920's *Outward Bound*. Significantly, this pessimistic dramatization of life-in-death provides *Steambath* with its central situation; but in *Happy Birthday, Wanda June* the "heaven" scenes, which contain hilarious characterizations, are incidental to the main plot and, alternating with scenes in the present, are resorted to for heightening of theatricality, change of pace, and variation in exposition. Both plays also query the nature of man, but Vonnegut's thesis about the absolescence of man-the-hunter is more sharply conceived and realized than Friedman's about man's ultimate ignorance of God. Vonnegut's man-as-killer is a palpable possibility for the stage, and it displays his instinctive sense of what is theatrically negotiable. Contrariwise, regardless of how wittily and audaciously Friedman wrestles with the problem of rendering God on stage in order to realize a maximum of dramatic effectiveness (for example, he uses the device of allowing the protagonist to question the validity of God's claims, thus voicing for the audience its own doubts), man-as-God resists human representation; God is an abstraction that suffers from banality when reduced to the visual, as even Milton discovered when he opposed an autocratic God to his indomitable Satan. In short, for those familiar with his novels, Vonnegut performs his usual prestidigitation, translating an ordinary observation into a vivid statement by means of his very personal (hence original) viewpoint; but Friedman proves to be at once conventional in his dramaturgy and quixotic in his demands on the resources of the theater and on the receptivity of the playgoer.

A tawdry New York City public steambath, presided over by a Puerto Rican attendant named Morty, is the setting. Neither hell nor heaven, the steambath is a purgatory-like stop for newly dead "Neurotics, freaks . . . those with stories to tell" (90) [14] before they are ushered through an onstage door to oblivion. There is no doubt about the Puerto Rican's pretensions to being God: he controls the world randomly between and during swipes of his mop by issuing orders to a bleeping electronic console, and he is careful to keep an even distribution between disasters and "good stuff" (28), even though the latter leaves him exhausted. As if to validate his credentials, he has a Jewish helper named Gottlieb (that is, he who loves God).

The action opens with the appearance of Tandy, a man between thirty-five and forty-five, who is initially puzzled by his surroundings. Slowly it dawns on him that he and the others in the steambath are dead. Most of the rest of the play is concerned (1) with his reluctance to accept the Puerto Rican as God and (2) with his refusal to accept his death. He challenges the Puerto Rican to prove his omnipotence. After the attendant commences with card tricks and magician's lock openings, he is forced by Tandy's skepticism into extravaganzas (such as gulping down a man-sized whiskey sour) and finally into an apocalyptic assertion of his divinity. The curtain falls on the first act with the steambath people kneeling before him as he ascends majestically to the highest tier of the room, his head crowned by celestial light, and his voice intoning, "ASCRIBE UNTO THE LORD YE KINDREDS OF THE PEOPLES . . . ASCRIBE UNTO THE LORD GLORY AND STRENGTH . . ." (45–46).

The second act presents a running debate between the Puerto Rican attendant and Tandy, who demands that he be returned to life or that his death be justified. Tandy argues that just before his arbitrary death he had gotten his "whole life on the right track for the first time . . . everything bad swept out of the room"

(85–86): he had accepted his ex-wife's infidelity and wished her well, he had rescued his mother from harsh work and settled her in an apartment in White Plains, he had quit his "art-appreciation job over at the Police Academy" (84), he had started writing a book on Charlemagne, he had "a marvelous new girl who's got this surprising body" (85), and he was "closer than ever" to his daughter (86). The Puerto Rican attendant's response is detached interest, with an occasional expression of surprise at Tandy's disclosure of an item he had not known.

In exasperation, Tandy insults the attendant with a blasphemy that both astonishes and outrages the attendant; but Tandy is unrepentant: "If you're capable of doing something like that," he replies, "Taking a fellow to the very threshold of marvelous things, teasing him along and then acing him out just when he's ready to scoop up one lousy drop of gravy—that is bad news, I'm sorry . . . Yeah, I'm going to stick to it" (89). Appearing to relent, the attendant asks Tandy what he would do if he were freed from the steambath. Tandy begins excitedly to tick off the activities of his new life style, of "the exciting world that's out there waiting'" for him (92). Seemingly innocent inquiries of the attendant deflect Tandy into long apologias admitting the hollowness and false motivation of his all-too-human desires. In short, Tandy reveals the emptiness and pointlessness of his life in the very process of his making a case for it. Friedman has created a scene dramatically convincing in its self-disclosure. The curtain falls with Tandy's cry, "I got to get out of here . . . I got to get out of here . . ."; but the Puerto Rican attendant impassively plays a game of solitaire, and the last sound heard, according to the stage directions, is *the flicking of the cards . . ."* (97).

As a piece of dramaturgy, *Steambath* is superior to *Scuba Duba*; for the control of place, situation, and dramatic structure is firmer. The expository details of Tandy's life—his resignation from a police academy job, his wife's infidelity with a film maker, his trip with his daughter, his mother's odd work habits—are spin-offs from *The Dick*.[15] This repetition reflects Friedman's creative limitations—or his delight in familiar material; yet the confrontation of Tandy and the Puerto Rican attendant marks a mature grasp of dramatic conflict. And Friedman's response to contemporary Americana, especially to the deterioration of life in its urban centers, is as sure as in the novels: the preoccupation of

New Yorkers with mugging and burglary, the Sears Roebuck mentality of Bloomingdale's, the pre-sliced lox of the delicatessens. He can deflate the sentimentalization of death by such homogenizing institutions of hucksterism as Forest Lawn with a deft allusion: "I thought dying meant that you'd have to spend every day of your life at a different Holiday Inn" (18). And he has learned to build repetition of phrasing into comic climaxes.

Above all, Friedman's representation of God in the play as a Puerto Rican steambath attendant is daring and imaginative. It neatly sidesteps the pitfall of banality which afflicts most gods who are necessarily decreased to life size on the stage. This God manages by means of the startling disjunction between his cultural status and his divine identity to suggest something of his nature: "Changeable, mysterious, infinite, unfathomable" (37)—but not without the deflation of laughter. For, in keeping with the attendant's appearance, he has a shocking naïveté and fallibility that rightly arouses Tandy's skepticism. He speaks mostly in the slangy, racy language of a denizen of Manhattan; but, when sorely tried by Tandy's scorn, he shifts into a comic-opera version of biblical speech—justifying the inconsistency of his rhetoric with the claim that "The Lord speaks in funny ways" (34). Tandy immediately raises objections: "I've heard of having your faith tested, but this is absurd" (37). And he is incredulous when his sneer at the attendant's card trick produces hurt feelings: "God with his feelings hurt. Ridiculous" (40). Nor does the attendant's cosmic system work perfectly at all times; he admits that he "can get any kind of food I want up here . . . except lox. The lox is lousy, pre-sliced . . . the kind you get in those German delicatessens . . . I can't get any fresh lox . . . I don't know why that is" (81). And he is not always omniscient. He admits to having missed Tandy's dying wish to live; but he shrugs it off with the lame explanation that "Once in a while there's an administrative error" (90).

What is the eventual effect of such a God on the playgoer? First, his arbitrariness stands out in large letters. Accused by Tandy of being unjust, the attendant jeers, "You're looking for fair, reasonable . . . where'd you get that from?" (73). At another point in their contest, he threatens Tandy, "You say another word, baby, I'll become wrathful and vengeance-seeking" (70). Second, Tandy must express the sentiments of the audience when he shouts in exasperation at the attendant, "I don't see God yet. Where's God?" (43).

The central thrust of the play sustains this statement about man's inability to recognize God—indeed, the silliness of his effort to comprehend even God's ways. If true, the age-old habits of propitiating God prove to be irrelevant. The steambath attendant corroborates this conclusion when he mocks Tandy's inquiry as to what he can do for the attendant: "You got to be kidding. *You* do something for *me?* What in the world would God want?" (88). Certainly, the attendant's inconsistencies of manner—by turn, bullying, quizzical, clownish, autocratic, ingratiating, indifferent, and eager to be believed—are not calculated to arouse man's hopes of mastering his ways. Man's pitiful attempts, past and present, to conceptualize omnipotence are laughed at in Friedman's tawdry portrayal of God's place and mode of operation in *Steambath*. And the Black Humor joke of parodying the traditional humble origins of Jesus by the lowly status of the Puerto Rican attendant underscores the feebleness of man's gesture to align himself with the divine unknown. The parodying of the spiritual exercise of the purgation of the soul with the cleansing of the body in a steambath likewise questions man's conception of the absolute.

Despite its successfully comic translation of sociotheological doubts into dramatic form, *Steambath* ultimately retains a residue of uncertainty as to the terms of the conflict. The play uneasily echoes earlier literary models associated with solemn religious values: the medieval debate over the salvation of the soul and the classic encounter in *Everyman* of man with death. These echoes give a literary and philosophical authenticity to Friedman's vision, but the triviality of Tandy's aspirations in life and of the attendant's demonstrations of omnipotence (he appears at first as if he were a vaudeville entertainer) are more reminiscent of the antics of Christoper Marlowe's Dr. Faustus than of the agonies of Goethe's Faust. In one of the most dramatic episodes, even the roles of man and God are reversed, thereby creating additional abscurity in an already vaporous atmosphere on stage. Tipped off by Gottlieb, Tandy has a fellow steambath inhabitant hold a mirror to the attendant's face. The attendant cringes away from his image. "Take that away," he cries, "I don't want to see myself. A homely guy with pockmarks" (91). Compassionately, Tandy deflects the mirror, unable to see the attendant in torment. "Et tu, Gottlieb," the Puerto Rican ripostes; and then he taunts Tandy, "You couldn't stand that, right, to see God get wiped out . . . It gave you a funny feeling" (91–92). The fairy-tale device of the mirror adds an inexplicable dimension of significance to the action, but the pointless allusion to Brutus' betrayal of Julius Caesar qualifies the seriousness with which we are asked to accept it. And, finally, the sudden suggestion that God is an expression of man's need to believe in omnipotence conflicts with the play's central assertion that God is beyond human comprehension.

Perhaps these details are meant to contribute to the thesis that man's notions of God are a compound of dime-store desires and preverbal myths. Yet, because of the shifts in tone and its blurrings of focus and cinema-like stoppings of the action, *Steambath* seems to be trying to make a larger statement than that. As in the writing of *Stern*, Friedman, who has reached deep into his subconscious for the materials of the play, shifts in ways not wholly clear to himself from his earlier obsession with the psychosocial and psychosexual to a new preoccupation with the sociotheological. That he is not sure of where this new direction may take him is reflected in a remark he made about *Steambath* during its composition. He acknowledged that he was at work on a full-length play "that I can't really tell about quite yet—much more experimental and outrageous than *Scuba Duba*—either very good or screamingly off-target—haven't the faintest idea." [16] There is some indication already that Friedman wrought more legitimately than he dared hope. *Steambath* was quickly added to the repertory of the nation's little theaters and has been staged among others by the Theater Now Repertory Troupe at the Century City Playhouse in Los Angeles during June and July, 1972, and has been produced for television and had several airings.

III   *Journalism*

Scuba Duba was a bright spot of the 1967–68 season, but its touring company oddly never attracted the interest or kudos that the New York production received. Film rights were sought avidly by Hollywood interests who routed Friedman out of bed in the middle of the night to talk lucrative deals before the play was finally optioned to Kenneth Hyman of Warner Bros–Seven Arts, Ltd. This success gave him breathing room financially to experiment with *Steambath* and to conclude *The Dick.* It also threw a new kind of distraction and temptation in his way. At fortyish he is, to an extent, at a crossroads in his career. He can go for the easy money thrust upon the "hot" writer by an America that always seems to be more avid to destroy than to nurture its literary talent—and he can become a comfortable—but anonymous—writer for the vast movie, television, and Broadway technostructure; or he can choose the perilous, lonely way of the novelist who wrote *Stern* and *A Mother's Kisses.* Friedman, himself, insists that he has a third option; for he has large ambitions. Nothing less than a man of letters in the European tradition is his goal—not just a novelist committed to a lonely vigil daily at his desk, nor a poet doing his private thing, nor a playwright transforming his personal life into public drama, but a man who engages in all three at one time or another, "who writes novels, plays, criticism, films, [and] items of journalism," as he remarked in an address to the American Studies Association of the Modern Language Association in December, 1966, on the subject "The American Writer as the Object of Public Attention." [17] European countries accept such versatility quite casually, he notes, yet "there is little American precedent" for this kind of career. Here, the writer is asked, "Why don't you give us another book like that first one?" Although Friedman continues to think of himself as a novelist and does not foresee the day when he would not have a novel in progress, he has striven "to become the American equivalent of the man of letters." The difficulties of flying in the face of the American admiration for the specialist has made Friedman openly sympathetic to the similar efforts of Norman Mailer, Truman Capote, and Terry Southern not to let themselves be confined by one genre.

Friedman's recent liaison with journalism is not a passion of the moment. It is the inevitable *affaire d'amour* of a flirtation that has continued off and on almost from prepuberty days. As a student of DeWitt Clinton High School, he wrote a column for *The Clinton News* called "AnyBuddy's Business," a self-conscious pun on his high-school nickname "Buddy." It was a natural step for him, then, when he enrolled in 1947 at the University of Missouri to major in journalism and, following his graduation in

1951, to work as correspondent, feature writer, and photographer on the Air Force magazine, *Air Training*, while serving as a non-flying officer in the United States Air Force for two years. He remembers *Air Training*, then edited by George Leonard, who was later with *Look* magazine, as "a real swinging magazine." "Under the influence of Max Shulman, I guess," he recalls, "I began writing some fables for it. Like: 'Pvt. So-and-So and His Fairy Sergeant.' It was wild stuff. The fairy sergeant had a wand made out of chopped liver, for example. But some of the fables did have all sorts of anti-establishment digs and got pretty nervous. Finally, some major general in Europe sent back a two-word cable: 'STOP FABLES.' So they leaned on us and that was it." [18]

By the time Friedman returned to New York in 1954, he had considerable experience in the media field. Newly married to a beautiful girl, Ginger Howard, whom he had met while stationed in St. Louis, he took a job with the Magazine Management Company, which publishes men's adventure magazines. Friedman eventually became editor of such publications as *Men, Male*, and *Man's World*. He stayed with Magazine Management for twelve years, coming home from his day's stint at the office and a two-and-a-half-hour trip to and from work to sneak in a few hours of writing after ten o'clock each night and on weekends. In that manner, he wrote three novels and thirty-odd short stories. The toll on Friedman in physical strength and nervous energy in these years was great. In the late 1950's, after three years of labor on a first novel appeared to have been in vain, he collapsed from exhaustion, requiring a long period of rest. He was able to pursue such a strenuous regimen for so long because, "I always felt comfortable at Magazine Management. I felt lucky not to be working, say, at Newsweek, in the world, using the same muscles." [19]

Despite the seeming antipathy between imaginative and non-imaginative writing implied in Friedman's explanation of why he was able to continue for so long leading a double literary existence, he argues that journalism is ordinarily a healthy variation in the novelist's normal occupation of "sitting around by himself in empty rooms and being sensitive." [20] Journalism offers a chance to circumvent his usual physical isolation and "to be in on the action, to see sectors of life I would otherwise know nothing about." [21] It may be a selfish argument, he admits; but, instead of lying back and fantasizing about fashion models, he actually sees some:

> Instead of having to imagine the Goldwater phenomenon, or allowing James Reston to imagine it for him in the N.Y. Times, a Norman Mailer gets to travel out and see the Republican convention first-hand. Instead of taking Yevtushenko's word for it, a Truman Capote gets to go to Russia and brings back what to my mind is the most moving and evocative work of journalism yet written on Russia. "The Muses Are Heard," a brilliant example of what can happen when the novelistic technique is turned loose on non-fiction. So journalism, once again, puts the novelist where the action is and perhaps, in some mysterious way—or in a direct way, the cases of Dostoevski and Hemingway—there is a powerful benefit ultimately to the writer's fictional work.[22]

Furthermore, as a social critic, Friedman finds great difficulty in dealing fictionally with the contemporary. "There is something in the day-to-day events in Vietnam, the Congo, Selma, that eludes the truly serious novelist, that resists serious fictional treatment." How can a novelist, he asks,

> compete with scenes of Walter Jenkins being caught at the YMCA trough by the CIA Urinal Squad. How can he concoct anything to compare with the Kennedy-Ruby-Oswald series of events. Whatever the case, through some chemistry that is difficult to analyse, something happens when the serious novelist dips into the immediate, contemporary. The novelist who alludes in his book to Jack Kennedy, to the Bay of Pigs, in some curious way runs the risk of spoiling the authority of what follows. And yet . . . you live in this world, you see things, react to them, are outraged and abashed, challenged by daily events—and . . . you need some ambiance, some channel, some outlet other than a patient wife. . . . For a really direct confrontation with whatever is on your mind, there is probably nothing better than the magazine piece.[23]

Much of Friedman's fiction draws directly on the tensions of his inner life and is hallucinatory in its felt vision. But his fiction relies equally for continued sustenance on his sensitivity to the current scene. In this respect, his journalism is an adjunct to his fiction; both probe the manic preoccupations of society. In the

mid-1960's, following publication of his two novels and a year
or so later by his resignation from Magazine Management Company, Friedman turned to journalism as a free-lance writer not
only for money in pocket but also for renewal of spirit and
restocking of mind. The essays that he wrote for *Esquire, Holiday,* and the *Saturday Evening Post* from 1965 to 1968 are sensitive re-creations of the folk heroes of the entertainment, sport,
and political worlds, who embody in almost mythic outline the
ideals that the rest of us palely ape.

Friedman published seven feature articles during those years,
beginning with a self-consciously camp description of "The Im-
posing Proportions of Jean Shrimpton" and a sly put-down of
"Raquel Welch: The Definitive Chickie" for *Esquire,* and ending
with a hard-eyed look at Joe Frazier's training regimen ("Will
Joe Frazier Be the Next Champ?") and an insouciant "exposé" of
"Adam Powell at the End of the World" for the *Saturday Evening
Post.* Two other essays, one on rock-and-roll bands ("The New
Sounds") and the other on Philadelphia disc-jockey Jerry Blavat
("The Number One Cat") demonstrate Friedman's sensitivity to
the faddish world of entertainment—his rapport with song and
dance, radio shows, and one-night stands reflects the peripheral
show-business associations of his boyhood. And an essay on the
daily routine of two Chicago homicide detectives, "Arrested by
Detectives Valesares and Sullivan, Charge: Murder," also for the
Saturday Evening Post, proves to be eerily prophetic of the civil
violence that flared at precinct level during the 1968 Democratic
National Convention.

Friedman's tone in these articles reflects his personal response
to experience, a combination of the child continually surprised
by the wonders of this brave new life and of the street gamin
born without illusions about human nature. His reaction to the
contrived world of mannequins and fashion, the frenetic scene
of rock and roll, and the discordant arenas of politics and law
enforcement partakes of the self-conscious awareness of the native New Yorker who preens himself on being nobody's fool.
Thus, his grasp of subject exhibits an imaginative totality absent
from most one-dimensional journalism. He can evoke the delicate
insubstantiality with which feminine beauty affects our senses,
as when he transmutes Jean Shrimpton into a "grmmphlett . . . a
mixture of baby giraffes and okapis and grysbok all mixed up into

one gracefully scattered Disney-Dr. Seuss thing," who, when startled, "begin a terrible feather-scattered gangling trot into the bush, the first clumsy thing they have ever done." [24] The underlying metaphor here—which becomes a leitmotif in the essay—of an African safari pinpoints as well the contrary dross of Jean Shrimpton's world: the predatory denizens of the fashion industry, the lecherous, tough-talking photographers and public relations agents who stalk their long-legged models with avid eye and cocked finger. As the product of dozens of people who haunt the fashion and advertising milieu, Jean Shrimpton is a made-up thing of arms, legs, and wigs. The *real* Jean Shrimpton, Friedman seems to be saying, is nonexistent—a make-believe grymmphlett!—a transubstantiated presence uncannily caught by the camera as a totality of being.

Friedman's ease in dealing with show business subjects is illustrated by his write-up of Raquel Welch. Its brevity—one page, flanked by photographs of the movie star in provocative poses— slyly implies that the subject lacks intellectual substance or conceptual weightiness, thereby underlining the narrow cinematic interests of Miss Welch, her crudely "hip " jargon, her limited version of herself as a cinematic commodity and of movie-making as an industry engaged in the promotion of money, lascivious "Living Legends," and eager but wary ingénues. Again, Friedman's literary instincts serve him well. He unabashedly confesses that only "private-eye-novel lingo" will do for describing Miss Welch: "a freshly poured torso, creamy breasts, legs that go on and on," a girl "hammered together" by a divine sport who decided, " 'This one gets to pick up all the marbles' and stamped her face forty per cent extra." [25] The verbs ("freshly poured," "hammered," "stamped") create an image of a manufactured product, thus confirming Miss Welch's vision of her astero-conception.

The same wedding of form and content characterizes Friedman's essays on Adam Clayton Powell and on the Chicago detectives Valesares and Sullivan. "Adam Powell at the End of the World" is substantially about Friedman's failure to get an interview with the controversial Negro politician, even though he had made a trip to Bimini and had lurked about the island for days. The article, then, subtly insinuates itself as an equivalent to the Harlem leader; for Friedman writes a self-serving, grandiose,

but essentially empty extravaganza. "Arrested by Detectives Valesares and Sullivan, Charge: Murder," contrariwise, concentrates
at extended length and in great detail on the day-to-day routine
of a big-city policeman—on the matter-of-fact dullness and bleak
repetitiveness of much of his work. And the structure of Friedman's reporting, almost minute by minute like a dramatization of
the radio and television show *Dragnet,* underscores the tension
of this endless sameness.

If Friedman is responsive to the inanity and superfluity of
contemporary existence, he is also cognizant of the violence that
is incipient in so much of the ordinary routine of modern urban
existence, the muted threat posed to the dull continuance of
things. This realization explains, in part, his attraction to boxing.
He does not transcendentalize a prize fight into a "clash between
Good and Evil, a carnival of existentialism," or into a "symbol of
rotting morality." He sees it "for what it is—two tough guys
beating each other up publicly so they can make some money
and allow us in the audience to indulge in a little vicarious violence." [26] Similarly, he diagnoses our acquiescence to sudden
motiveless fury on the streets of America as a sinister corollary
to our bizarre confusion of detective crime tales with the real
thing. Television and the movies have so saturated us that we
unwittingly adjust our sensibilities to the accepted electronic
response. Unfortunately, in this reverse of the notion that art follows life, the smell of mayhem does not survive the trip from
life to the actors to the camera across the television tubes into
the living room.

Ironically, Friedman notes that he succumbed to the same
blurring of the sharp details of life as he followed Valesares and
Sullivan on their workaday round: "I had been working with
Pete and John in an atmosphere of death and tragedy and had
somehow never really made contact with the reality of what
I had been observing." Then one day when he accompanies them
to the target range and watches "John's deliberate style of shooting at the bull's eye that might have been Teeth," he suddenly
sees the situation for what it is: "For all their very real and easy-
going charm, for all of the breakfast-show comedy and the New
Breed accounting-executive styles, they were basically tough men
in a bleak world the color of gun metal where grief and misery
make up the day's workload." [27] A writer can hardly pinpoint

more effectively the "imaginary gardens with real toads in them" [28] that the urban jungles of our cities have become.

Friedman's journalistic style differs little from the "hip" jargons and rock rhythms of contemporary subcultures to which his fiction is attuned. In this consistency of voice he substantiates his conviction about the sense of responsibility and the validity of purpose with which the man of letters executes his multiform writing chores. Such a professional does his best whether it is a magazine article or the Great American Story. "I think it's an attitude," he avers, "that says I have only one hat, one voice, a writer's voice, my own voice—and that no matter what I do—a safety jingle, a sonnet, a song lyric, a 1000-page monologue, a panel for Famous Funnies or a letter to Aunt Bertha, I will do it only one way and that is, with all the power and vigor and skill at my command." [29]

Friedman's journalistic prose is a flexible instrument, comparable in its effectiveness to the prose of such literary journalists as Norman Mailer and Terry Southern, but it is less baroque than Mailer's and more verbally equivalent to its frenetic subject than Southern's. It has a spontaneous air of being written on the run, reportorial fashion, notebook and pencil in hand while in hot pursuit of the story. Yet this language—dense with verbs, nouns, proper names, hyphenated words—jangling, jarring, eliptical, is highly stylized, carefully constructed by Friedman, who neither talks nor thinks in such staccato rhythms. With admirable precision he adjusts this prose to the demands of the subject matter. Thus, in contrast to the lyrical swing of the sentences describing Jean Shrimpton's "grmmphlett" diffidence, the prose description in "The New Sounds" of rock and roll takes on verbal density. Alternately violent and sweet, soft and blaring at full decibel count, it evokes the sound tunnel of pop music, its solipsistic lyrics, and its engulfing waves of percussive rhythm.

Or we have Friedman's characterization of one of the phenomenons of the 1960's, the under-thirty czars of the rock-and-roll record industry: "Crewe, a shade under thirty, sits in an elaborate fanback chair and there is executive hold-my-calls, and show-Mr-so-and-so-in, yet when he puts on a record for you (*Dusty,* by the Rag Dolls) as loud as you have ever heard one played, and the room fills up with the Bob Crewe sound—you walk around inside the music, elbowing aside deep chords, ducking a suddenly flung falsetto note—he is suddenly young, totally engaged, a finger-snapping, foot-tapping, turned-on moaner and lip-biter. . . ." [30] And here is Friedman on the social implications of the current rage among teen-agers for rock music: "Some of the groups are chaotic, cannibal-like, unruly gangs, just moving and shouting, really, as if to drown out the massive Jack Ruby chord of absurdity that has been struck in the land." [31]

This writing is reporting at its best: emotionally seismographic in a responsible but subjective way to the nuances, the underground reverberations, that announce new volcanic formations of culture. In these articles, Friedman earns a place beside Mailer, Vonnegut, Southern, Baldwin, and the others of the new breed of writers who add a fresh, subjective strata to journalism.

Nor is Friedman's journalistic writing a sometime bread-and-butter thing of the past. During the first half of 1971, with his third novel just published and his second play just produced, he took a breather from imaginative writing to compose a series of articles for *Esquire, Harper's,* and *Playboy.* The first to appear was "Dirty Pictures, Dig? (Yes, Dig)," [32] an illustrated commentary on the earth world of Michael Heizer, Robert Smithson, Dennis Oppenheim, and Walter De Maria. In the course of his remarks, Friedman broaches the question of how, as art, such environmental "sculptures" can be marketed and esthetically evaluated. With acumen, he notes that these sculptures in their alteration of the earth's surface challenge the cosmos, but do not try to depict it. Such an observation is in line with his new interest in things teleological, as dramatized in *Steambath.*

The subsequent articles, though, indicate that Friedman in his concern for ultimate questions of life and death has not lost touch with the stranger-than-fiction happenings of the mid-twentieth century. His fascination with the seamy world of crime continues in his chronicle of several days in the life of a big-city detective, "Lessons of the Street," [33] which lampoons a paranoic proclivity of the plainclothes cop to read sinister implications in apparently innocent activities on the streets of Manhattan; and in his review, "Requiem for a Heavy," [34] of the mystery—whether by natural causes as the official police version states or by an overdose of heroin as rumor and circumstantial evidence has it—of how Sonny Liston met his death several years ago in Las Vegas. No less focused on death is Friedman's portrait in "Art of

Autopsy" [35] of the Los Angeles coroner Thomas T. Noguchi, who performed the autopsies on Robert Kennedy, Janis Joplin, and the Tate murder victims among others and who figured in a recent sensational hearing in which he successfully defended himself against charges of incompetence and insanity. More lighthearted is Friedman's sympathetic interview, "Why Won't Jackie Onassis Leave Galella Alone?" [36] of the American paparazzo Ron Galella, who has taken almost 4000 unauthorized pictures of Jackie Kennedy Onassis over the last five years; and his mock-serious inquiry, "Look, Mao, I'm Dancing," [37] into the alleged victory dance of the Tanzanians on the floor of the U.N. General Assembly when Taiwan was voted out of membership. These articles demonstrate that journalism continues to offer Friedman a change of writing pace—a relief from his more arduous creative writing— and to feed his creative thought.

Conclusion: *Bruce Jay Friedman: The Man in the Writing*

Those who wish to read Bruce Jay Friedman in place of Stern, Joseph, and Harold Wonder—and his mother in place of Meg— are not wholly wrong. Friedman does draw deeply on his past; indeed, he cheerfully admits doing so. But he gives us no direct transcription of the details of his life as does Thomas Wolfe in so much of his writing. Friedman is not ultimately Stern because he is at all times more than the sum of Stern. Friedman remains faithful to the psychological ambience of his experience while translating it into events that have wider social application for our times. He is in a sense, like Mark Twain, inventing himself through his creative memory; and thus he is shaping in a remarkable way his own personal myth, one which serves at the same time as a distillation of one kind of social experience in mid-century urban America.

His tales dwell on the random social violence of our times. His heroes are frightened conformists beset on all sides by the hieroglyphs of our supermarket culture, and they come of age in an ambience of devouring virago mothers, of inconstant wives, of racial conflict, and of computerized anonymity. They are betrayed by giveaway promotional schemes inflated to cosmic and vaguely supernatural proportions. The erotic props of bust and buttocks

entice them into empty daydreams that leave only the stale after-
taste of anticipated sin on their lips. Friedman's fictional creations are thus less authentic individuals than, as one reviewer
has noted, "the composite disturbed Everyman" [38] of the American technological revolution of the post-World-War-II era. Filled
with angst, they burrow through a steel and concrete jungle
like some species of primordial beings, evolutionary forms of a
new geological age, condemned to an environment of smog,
radioactive rain, polluted lakes and rivers, and high-decibel
mechanical noises.

Friedman's fiction is, therefore, the response of a sensitive individual to America at mid-century—to a culture defined by the
movies and television, by billboards and flashing neon signs, by
psychology textbooks and pornographic paperbacks, by Dr. Spock
and David Riesman, by assassinations and the Vietnam War, by
the electronic invasion of the home, and by the super megapolis.
Despite their characteristics of Black Humor, his stories are
parables of discovery. In the talk that Friedman gave at Coe
College, he distinguished between the Realistic writer, "who
knows everything when he begins," and the non-Realistic writer
of postwar fiction, who "uses the very props of madness and
often absurdity to analyze the madness and absurdity of the
current world." "More befuddled than the documentary writer,"
the non-Realist responds like a "fragile but unerring litmus paper
to the ills and inequities about him. . . . It is this latter breed of
writer who sets out on a voyage with no clear destination, who
simply allows himself to be steered by the hot and frenzied winds
of his imagination, who makes discoveries in an innocent trance,
who not only feeds the work but gets fed by it." This concept
of the writer (which accurately describes Friedman's brand of
artistic courage) as one embarked on a "mapless voyage" might
easily be mistaken for Wordsworth's description in *The Prelude*
of the poet's response to the world about him. In Friedman's use
of fiction as a means of discovering and defining himself, he is
clearly in the Romantic tradition. At the same time, because of
his preoccupation in his fiction with the identity of the century's
Massenmensch, he is recognizably a writer of the mid-twentieth
century.

This dependency on instinct and on the stream of experience
suggests that Friedman's vision and talents may be circumscribed

by the limiting focus of private obsessions and of temporal circumstances. There is a disturbing repetitiveness in his conception
of Stern-Joseph-Harold Wonder and of LePeters-Tandy; of
Stern's, Harold's, LePeters', and Tandy's mothers; and of all the
protagonists' fathers. Great novelists, such as Dickens and Faulkner, have traditionally had a seemingly inexhaustible capacity for
the creation of character. But Friedman seemingly lacks such
imaginative inventiveness. However, he has yet to tackle a large
canvas—has yet to conceive on the scale of even a Bellow or a
Mailer.

It may be unfair to judge Friedman according to the special
desiderata of the novelist because, although Friedman is a serious
inventor of stories, his ambitions as a writer embrace a wider
concept than the narrow focus of the novelist alone. Indeed, he
appears most recently to be concentrating on writing for the
theater, for he is at work in collaboration with Jacques Levy on
a third play tentatively entitled *First Offenders.*

Friedman seems to be trying to realize in the area of letters
the exhilarating range of competence and achievement that
Leonard Bernstein managed in music for so many years. It is
still too early to know whether he will be able to bring off such
an audacious ambition. Bruce Jay Friedman is still young enough,
still graced with sufficient physical strength and with intellectual
valor, to enable him to hit "a long ball" (as his friend Norman
Mailer put it in another context) into the accelerated hurricane
air of American letters.

Notes and References

Chapter One

1. Bruce Jay Friedman, Foreword, *Black Humor* (New York, 1965), pp. x-xi. The same essay with slight changes appears as "Those Clowns of Conscience" in *Book Week*, II (July 18, 1965), 2, 7.

2. *Ibid.*, pp. vii-viii. I have quoted here from the version in *Book Week*.

3. *Ibid.*, p. xi.

4. Robert Scholes, *The Fabulators* (New York, 1967), pp. 35–46.

5. Conrad Knickerbocker, "Humor with a Mortal Sting," *New York Times Book Review*, LXIX, Pt. 2 (September 27, 1964), 3, 60–61; cf. Richard Schickel, "The Old Critics and the New Novel," *Wisconsin Studies in Contemporary Literature*, V (1964), 26–36.

6. Richard Kostelanetz similarly wishes to place the American novel of the absurd in an antirealistic fablist tradition in "The American Absurd Novel," *The World of Black Humor*, ed. Douglas M. Davis (New York, 1967), pp. 306–13; originally published as "The Point Is That Life Doesn't Have Any Point, *New York Times Book Review*, LXX (June 6, 1965), 3, 28–30.

7. *English Institute Essays 1948* (New York, 1949), pp. 58–73; reprinted in *Theories of Comedy*, ed. Paul Lauter (New York, 1964), pp. 450–60, from which I quote.

8. Marcus Klein, *After Alienation: American Novels in Mid-Century* (New York, 1964).

9. William Sherman, "J. P. Donleavy: Anarchic Man as Dying Dionysian," *Twentieth Century Literature*, XIII (1968), 216.

10. Bruce Jay Friedman, *Black Humor*, p. viii.

11. Louis-Ferdinand Céline, *Journey to the End of the Night* (New York, 1960), pp. 459, 504. All subsequent references are to this edition.

12. William Godwin, *An Enquiry Concerning Political Justice* (1793), bk. II, ch. 2.

13. Thomas Pynchon, "Journey into the Mind of Watts," *New York Times Magazine* (June 12, 1966), p. 84.

14. *Stern* (New York, 1962), p. 191.

15. Knickerbocker, "Humor with a Mortal Sting," p. 61.

16. Northrop Frye, "The Argument of Comedy," *Theories of Comedy*, p. 453.

17. Scholes, *The Fabulators*, p. 43.

18. Knickerbocker, "Humor with a Mortal Sting," p. 61.

19. Cf. Robert Garis, "What Happened to John Barth?" *Commentary*, LXXXV (October, 1966), 80–82; Earl Rovit, "The Novel as Parody: John Barth, *Critique*, VI (1963); 77–85; John M. Muste, "Better to Die Laughing: The War Novels of Joseph Heller and John Ashmead," *Critique*, V (1962), 16–17; and John Wain, "A New Novel about Old Troubles," *Critical Quarterly*, V (1963), 168–73.

20. Knickerbocker, "Humor with a Mortal Sting," p. 60.

21. *Black Humor*, p. xi.

22. *A Mother's Kisses* (New York, 1964), pp. 14–15; henceforth referred to as *Kisses*.

23. Richard Kostelanetz, "The American Absurd Novel," *The World of Black Humor*, p. 309.

24. Robert Buckeye, "The Anatomy of the Psychic Novel," *Critique*, IX (1965), 33–34.

25. John Enck, "John Barth: An Interview," *Wisconsin Studies in Contemporary Literature*, VI (1965), 3–14.

26. Alfred Appel, "*Lolita*: The Springboard of Parody," *Wisconsin Studies in Contemporary Literature*, VIII (1967), 237.

27. Interview by me with Bruce Jay Friedman, December 30, 1967.

28. John Barth, "The Literature of Exhaustion," *The Atlantic*, CCXX (August, 1967), 29–34. Borges has written that "The Baroque is that style which deliberately exhausts (or tries to exhaust) its possibilities and borders on its own caricature"; quoted in *Labyrinths* (Norfolk, Conn., 1962), p. xxii.

29. Douglas M. Davis, *The World of Black Humor*, p. 30.

30. Barth, "The Literature of Exhaustion," p. 34.

31. Knickerbocker, "Humor with a Mortal Sting," p. 61.

Chapter Two

1. Norman Mailer, *The Presidential Papers* (New York, 1963), pp. 38–39.

2. Cf. Martin Levin, *New York Times Book Review*, LXVII (September 23, 1962), 44; Stanley Edgar Hyman, "An Exceptional First Novel," *The New Leader*, XLV (October 1, 1962), 22–23; Jeremy Larner, "Compulsion to Toughness," *The Nation*, CXCV (December 1, 1962), 380–81; Nat Hentoff, "Anxiety and Paranoia," *Commonweal*, LXXVII (December 7, 1962), 294–95; and Nelson Algren, "The Radical Innocent," *The Nation*, CXCIX (September 1, 1964), 142–43.

3. All citations are to Bruce Jay Friedman, *Stern* (New York, 1962).

4. I am deeply indebted in this section to an unpublished study of *Stern* made by Dr. Paul Kay of Great Neck, Long Island. Although I disagree with Dr. Kay's interpretation of the outcome of Stern's actions, I find his fully documented discussion of the psychoerotic ambience of Judaism and of its links with puberty rites instructive and seminal. For acute but undeveloped intuitions in the same direction, see the reviews of *Stern* by Alfred Chester, "Submitting, Not Rising to the Heroic Gesture," New York *Herald Tribune Books* (September 23, 1962), p. 8; and Stanley Edgar Hyman, "An Exceptional First Novel," *The New Leader*, XLV (October 1, 1962), 22–23.

5. Cf. Joshua Trachtenberg, *Jewish Magic and Superstition* (New York, 1939); Andrew Peto, "The Demonic Mother Imago in the Jewish Religion," *Psychoanalysis and the Social Sciences*, ed. Warner Muensterberger and Sidney Alexrod (New York, 1958) V, 280–86; Geza Roheim, "Some Aspects of Semitic Monotheism," *Psychoanalysis and the Social Sciences*, ed. Walter Muensterberger and Sidney Axelrod (New York, 1955), IV, 169–217.

6. Cf. Ernest Jones, "The Psychology of the Jewish Question," *Essays in Applied Psychoanalysis* (London, 1951), I, 284–300; Rudolf M. Lowenstein, *Christians and Jews* (New York, 1963), p. 134; Theodore Reik, *Masochism in Modern Man*, trans. Margaret H. Beigel (New York, 1941); and C. G. Montefiore and H. Loewe, *Rabbinic Anthology* (Philadelphia 1960), pp. 93, 541–55.

7. Hannah Arendt, *Eichmann in Jerusalem* (New York, 1963); cf. also Max L. Margoles and Alexander Marks, *A History of the Jewish People* (New York, 1965).

8. According to Theodore Lidz and Robert Rubinstein, "Psychology of Gastro Intestinal Disorders," *The American Handbook of Psychiatry,* ed. Arieti Sylvano (New York, 1950), I, 683–84; and Angel Garma, "On the Pathogenesis of Peptic Ulcer," *The International Journal of Psychoanalysis*, XXXI (1950), 53–71; peptic ulcers in men are frequently accompanied by feminine identification, close attachment to the mother, and strong latent homosexuality.

9. Dr. Paul Kay believes that *Stern* portrays a more successful outcome of its protagonist's struggle to assume an adult paternal identity than I am willing to allow. He interprets Stern's damaged ear as not only representative of "a new conscience and sense of identity and a new way of life" but also a "token castrative punishment for his sexual wishes towards his mother" and hence "a sign of his new masulinity" (pp. 10–11).

10. Bruce Jay Friedman, *Black Humor* (New York, 1965), p. x.

11. Alfred Tennyson, *In Memoriam*, LVI.

12. William Wordsworth, *The Prelude*, VII, 722, 726.

13. *Selected Stories of Sholom Aleichem,* ed. Alfred Kazin (New York, 1965), p. ix.

Chapter Three

1. All citations are to Bruce Jay Friedman, *A Mother's Kisses* (New York, 1964).

2. Bruce Jay Friedman, *Steambath* (New York, 1971), pp. 61–62.

3. Norman Mailer, *Cannibals and Christians* (New York, 1966), p. 128.

4. Cf. Josh Greenfield, "Bruce Jay Friedman Is Hanging by His Thumbs," *New York Times Magazine* (January 14, 1968), pp. 36, 41.

5. Interview by me with Bruce Jay Friedman, December 30, 1967.

6. *Ibid.*

7. According to Samuel Irving Bellman, "The 'Jewish Mother' Syndrome," *Congress Bi-Weekly,* XXXII (December 27, 1965), 3–5, the conventions include "conspicuous self-sacrifice combined with incessant demands for attention," "the tendency to force-feed her children," "the habit of universal complaint," "paranoid egomania," and "a deep-rooted obsession in regard to the welfare and obedience of the children" (3). So concentrated on the "Jewish Mother" syndrome is Bellman, however, that he overlooks the real divergences of Meg from the type, unwarrantly tagging her as a "man-eating Mother" (3).

8. Interview by me with Bruce Jay Friedman, December 30, 1967.

Chapter Four

1. All citations are to *Far from the City of Class* (New York, 1963), henceforth referred to as *City Class,* and to *Black Angels* (New York, 1966).

2. Quoted by Josh Greenfield, "Bruce Jay Friedman Is Hanging by His Thumbs," *New York Times Magazine* (January 14, 1968), p. 38.

3. Samuel I. Bellman, "Old Pro" [Review of *Black Angels*], *Congress Bi-Weekly,* XXXIV (May 8, 1967), p. 19.

4. *Ibid.*

5. Samuel I. Bellman, review of *Far from the City of Class,* in *Studies in Short Fiction,* I (1963–64), 167.

6. Louis D. Rubin, Jr., *The Curious Death of the Novel: Essays in American Literature* (Baton Rouge, 1967), p. 15.

Chapter Five

1. All citations are to Bruce Jay Friedman, *The Dick* (New York, 1970).

2. Alexander Welsh, *The Hero of the Waverley Novels* (New Haven, 1963).

3. *Coleridge's Miscellaneous Criticism,* ed. Thomas M. Raysor (Cambridge, Mass., 1936), p. 335.

4. I am indebted in the following pages to Wylie Sypher's perceptive discussion (in *Loss of the Self in Modern Literature and Art* [New York, 1962]) of the ironical contradiction of aims in the nineteenth century between the Romantic assertion of the self and the liberal ideal of the greatest good for the greatest number.

5. For an acute evaluation of the sensibility of much modern art, see Saul Bellow, "Some Notes on Recent American Fiction," *Encounter,* XXI (1963), 22–29.

Chapter Six

1. Clive Barnes, *New York Times* (October 11, 1967), p. 36. For consistently hostile views, see Richard Gilman's two articles, "Anatomy of a Hit," *The New Republic,* CLVII (October 28, 1967), 31–33, and "Who Needs Critics?" *The New Republic,* CLVIII (February 17, 1968), 25–26. Also see Paine Knickerbocker's adverse comments when the play opened with a second company in San Francisco at the Alcazar-on-Broadway, August 6, 1968: "Race and a Cuckold," San Francisco *Chronicle* (August 8, 1968), p. 44; and "I Never Answer Critics, But This Time I'm Mad; Really Mad: And So . . ." San Francisco Sunday *Examiner and Chronicle* (August 25, 1968), Datebook, p. 3.

2. Quoted by Josh Greenfield, "Bruce Jay Friedman Is Hanging by His Thumbs," *New York Times Magazine* (January 14, 1968), p. 36.

3. *Ibid.,* p. 42.

4. *Ibid.,* p. 41.

5. *Ibid.,* p. 41.

6. Leslie A. Fiedler, "Indian or Injun," *Waiting for the End* (New York, 1964), pp. 113–14.

7. All citations are to the printed version, Bruce Jay Friedman, *Scuba Duba* (New York, 1967).

8. Also noted by Clive Barnes, *New York Times* (October 11, 1967), p. 36.

9. My Interview with Bruce Jay Friedman, December 30, 1967.

10. Richard Gilman, "Who Needs Critics?" *The New Republic,* CLVIII (February 17, 1968), p. 25.

11. Richard Gilman, "Anatomy of a Hit," *The New Republic,* CLVII (October 28, 1967), pp. 32–33.

12. My interview with Bruce Jay Friedman, December 30, 1967.

13. Quoted by Paine Knickerbocker, San Francisco *Chronicle* (August 6, 1968), p. 39.

14. All citations are to the printed version, Bruce Jay Friedman, *Steambath.*

15. The first printed version of some of this material appears in the uncollected short story "The Partners," *Esquire*, LXXII (August, 1969), 72–74, 150–52.

16. From a letter of March 22, 1969, by Bruce Jay Friedman to me.

7. In addition to the American Studies Association address, entitled "What Happens When the Writer Becomes a Public Figure?," Friedman gave talks at Coe College and at the University of North Carolina in 1966 and 1967. The latter address was part of an *Esquire* Symposium, which also had as participants Isaac Bashevis Singer, Norman Podhoretz, and Jack Richardson. All three lectures (to date unpublished) are concerned with the novelist as journalist: specifically with the relationship of journalism to fiction and with the appeal of non-fictional writing to the novelist.

18. Quoted by Josh Greenberg, "Bruce Jay Friedman Is Hanging by His Thumbs," *New York Times Magazine* (January 14, 1968), p. 38.

19. *Ibid.*

20. Speech on "The Fiction Writer as Journalist or Critic of Society," given at Coe College.

21. *Ibid.*

22. Speech on "The Appeals of Non-Fictional Writing," given at the University of North Carolina.

23. *Ibid.*

24. "The Imposing Proportions of Jean Shrimpton," *Esquire*, XLIII (April, 1965), 72.

25. "Raquel Welch: The Definitive Chickie," *Esquire*, LXIV (October, 1965), 85.

26. "Will Joe Frazier Be the Next Champ?" *Saturday Evening Post*, CCXL (September 23, 1967), 98.

27. "Arrested by Detectives Valesares and Sullivan, Charge: Murder," *Saturday Evening Post*, CCXL (April 22, 1967), 47.

28. Marianne Moore, "Poetry," Stanza 5.

29. Speech on "The Appeals of Non-Fictional Writing."

30. "The New Sounds," *Holiday*, XXXVIII (July, 1965), 102.

31. *Ibid.*, p. 44.

32. "Dirty Pictures, Dig? (Yes, Dig)," *Esquire*, LV (May, 1971), 112–17, 42.

33. "Lessons of the Street," *Harper's*, CCXLIII (September, 1971), 86–95.

34. "Requiem for a Heavy," *Esquire*, LXXVI (August, 1971), 54–57, 118–20.

35. "Art of Autopsy," *Esquire*, LXXVI (December, 1971), 96–106.

36. "Why Won't Jackie Onassis Leave Calella Alone?" *Esquire*, LXXVII (March, 1972), 94–95, 166–69.

37. "Look, Mao, I'm Dancing," *Esquire*, LXXVII (April, 1972), 55, 58.

38. Webster Schott, New York *Times Book Review*, LXXI (October 2, 1966), 4.

Selected Bibliography

PRIMARY SOURCES

1. *Novels*

   Stern. New York: Simon and Schuster, Inc., 1962.
   A Mother's Kisses. New York: Simon and Schuster, Inc., 1964.
   The Dick. New York: Alfred A. Knopf, 1970.

2. *Short Stories*

   Far from the City of Class. New York: Frommer-Pasmantier, 1963.
   Contains "For Your Viewing Entertainment," "Far from the
   City of Class," "When You're Excused You're Excused," "The
   Trip," "A Foot in the Door," "The Subversive," "The Little
   Ball," "Mr. Prinzo's Breakthrough," "The Good Time," "The
   Man They Threw Out of Jets," "Wonderful Golden Rule Days,"
   "The Holiday Celebrators," "Yes, We Have No Ritchard," "The
   Big Six," "The Canning of Mother Dean," and "23 Pat O'Brien
   Movies."
   Black Angels. New York: Simon and Schuster, Inc., 1966. Contains
   "Black Angels," "The Punch," "The Investor," "The Operator,"
   "Brazzaville Teen-ager," "A Change of Plan," "The Interview,"
   "Show Biz Connections," "The Enemy," "The Death Table,"
   "The Night Boxing Ended," "The Neighbors," "The Hero,"
   "Let Me See Faces," "The Mission," and "The Humiliation."

3. *Drama*

   Scuba Duba. New York: Simon and Schuster, Inc., 1967.
   Steambath. New York: Alfred A. Knopf, 1971.

4. *Journalism*

   "The Imposing Proportions of Jean Shrimpton," *Esquire*, LXIII
   (April, 1965), 70–75, 148–50.
   "The New Sounds," *Holiday*, XXXVIII (July, 1965), 44–45, 98,
   102.
   "Those Clowns of Conscience," *Book Week*, II (July 18, 1965), 2, 7.

"Raquel Welch: The Definitive Chickie," *Esquire,* LXIV (October, 1965), 84–87, 166.

"What's in It for Me," *Harper's,* CCXXXI (November, 1965), 168–69.

"Keep Out of My Hair," *Saturday Evening Post,* CXXIX (January 15, 1966), 6, 10.

"The Number One Cat," *Saturday Evening Post,* CCXXIX (September 24, 1966), 36–42.

"Céline," *New York Times Book Review,* LXXII (February 5, 1967), 1, 52.

"Arrested by Detectives Valesares and Sullivan, Charge: Murder," *Saturday Evening Post,* CCXL (April 22, 1967), 38–47.

"Adam Powell at the End of the World," *Saturday Evening Post,* CCXL (May 20, 1967), 26–29.

Will Joe Frazier Be the Next Champ?" *Saturday Evening Post,* CCXL (September 23, 1967), 97–101.

" 'Don't Dare Put Me in Your Play!' " *The Writer,* LXXXII (June, 1969), 16–18; reprinted from *Playbill* (October, 1968).

"Dirty Pictures, Dig? (Yes, Dig)," *Esquire,* LXXV (May, 1971), 112–17, 42.

"Requiem for a Heavy," *Esquire,* LXXVI (August, 1971), 54–57, 118–20.

"Lessons of the Street," *Harper's,* CCXLIII (September, 1971), 86–95.

"Art of Autopsy,"*Esquire,* LXXVI (December, 1971), 96–106.

"Why Won't Jackie Onassis Leave Galella Alone?" *Esquire,* LXXVII (March, 1972), 94–95, 166–69.

"Look, Mao, I'm Dancing," *Esquire,* LXXVII (April, 1972), 55, 58.

SECONDARY SOURCES

1. *Criticism of Friedman's Writings*

Algren, Nelson. "The Radical Innocent," *The Nation,* CXCIX (September 21, 1964), 142–43. A pioneering estimate of Friedman's talents.

Bellman, Samuel I. "Old Pro," *Congress Bi-Weekly,* XXXIV (May 8, 1967), 19. A review of *Black Angels,* with a suggestive analysis of Friedman's treatment of the theme of a *quid-pro-quo* covenant between a worried, insecure individual and a satanic, regulative higher Power.

Chester, Alfred. "Submitting, Not Rising to the Heroic Gesture," New York *Herald Tribune Books* (September 23, 1962), p. 8. Suggestive remarks about the conformist, unheroic qualities of

Stern and about Friedman's limitations as a creator of fictional characters.

Gilman, Richard. "Oedipus, Shmedipus, Mama Loves You," *Book Week*, I (August 23, 1964), 5, 8. Review of *A Mother's Kisses* contains acute references to Friedman's comic gifts.

――――. "Antamony of a Hit," *The New Republic*, CLVII (October 28, 1967), 31–33. "Who Needs Critics?" *The New Republic*, CLVIII (February 17, 1968), 25–26. Hostile but thoughtful discussions of the "New Barbarism" in contemporary literature, apropos of the "jerry-built" style and form of *Scuba Duba.*

Greenfield, Josh. "Bruce Jay Friedman Is Hanging by His Thumbs," *New York Times Magazine* (January 14, 1968), pp. 30–42. Survey of Friedman as the New York theater success of 1967; includes some interesting biographical information.

Hicks, Granville. "Domestic Felicity?" *Saturday Review*, XLIX (September 24, 1966), 31–32. Review of *Black Angels;* some consideration of Friedman's use of fantasy as a way of apprehending reality and of Friedman's willingness to take risks.

Hyman, Stanley Edgar. "An Exceptional First Novel," *The New Leader*, XLV (October 1, 1962), 22–23. Judicious formulation, mostly Freudian, of Stern's sexual complexes and neuroses.

Kaplan, Charles. "Escape into Hell: Friedman's *Stern,*" *California English Journal* (1965), 25–30. Discusses the Jewish theme as a version of the theme of alienation and of the antihero in contemporary American fiction.

Kauffmann, Stanley. "Frightened Writer," *The New Republic*, CLV (October 8, 1966), 20–37. Questionable statements about the psychic urges behind Friedman's writing; excellent comments on Friedman's Black Humor.

Larner, Jeremy. "Compulsion to Toughness," *The Nation*, CXCV (December 1, 1962), 380–81. Sympathetic case for the realism of Friedman's fantasy in *Stern.*

Klein, Marcus. "Further Notes on the Dereliction of Culture," *Contemporary American-Jewish Literature: Critical Essays*, ed. Irving Malin (Bloomington, Indiana, 1973), pp. 229–47. Discusses the peculiar authoritativeness of the novels in isolating and developing as clichés the terrifying ordinariness of social disintegration and of domestic dissolution.

Numasawa, Koji. "Everyman/Schlemiel," *Eigo Seinen* (Tokyo), CXIV (1968), 516–17. Discussion ranges from Thurber's Mitty to Friedman's Stern.

Schulz, Max F. "Edward Lewis Wallant and Bruce Jay Friedman: The Glory and the Agony of Love," *Critique*, X (1968), 31–

47. Studies of Friedman's depiction of love and sex in his two novels.

————. "Pop, Op, and Black Humor: The Aesthetics of Anxiety," *College English*, XXX (1968), 230–41. Analysis of the conformist hero in contemporary fiction; Friedman's novels supply major illustrations.

————. "Toward a Definition of Black Humor," *The Southern Review*, IX (1973), 117–34. Discussion of the origins of Black Humor and of its pluralistic view of the universe; the principal focus is on Friedman and his writings.

————. "The Aesthetics of Anxiety; and, the Conformist Heroes of Bruce Jay Friedman and Charles Wright," *Black Humor Fiction of the Sixties: A Pluralistic Definition of Man and His World* (Athens, Ohio, 1973), pp. 91–123. Studies of Friedman's depiction of modern man as conformist in mid-twentieth-century American society.

Index

FINKELSTEIN MEMORIAL LIBRARY

78-05350

813   SCHULZ, MAX
54   BRUCE JAY FRIEDMAN
FRIEDMAN

DATE			

FINKELSTEIN
MEMORIAL LIBRARY
SPRING VALLEY, N. Y.

© THE BAKER & TAYLOR CO.

JAN 18 1978